Reasserting the Disney Brand in the Streaming Era

Reasserting the Disney Brand in the Streaming Era investigates the evolution of the Disney brand at a pivotal moment – the move from content creation to acquisition and streaming – and how the company reasserted its brand in a changing marketplace.

Exploring how Disney's acquisition of Pixar, Marvel, Lucasfilm, and Fox positioned the company to launch the Disney+ streaming service, the chapters look at the history of those acquisitions, and the deployment of the content, brands, and intellectual property from those acquisitions, through an analysis of the original content that appeared on Disney+. Offering a focused investigation of how the content offered from these various media brands was adapted for Disney+ so that it reflects the Disney brand, the authors illustrate through close textual analysis how this content reflects elements of the "Classic Disney Style." The analysis positions these texts in relation to their industrial contexts, while also identifying important touchstone texts (both television and film) in Disney's catalog.

This comprehensive and thoughtful analysis will interest upper-level students and scholars of media studies, political economy, Disney studies, media industries, and new technology.

Robert Alan Brookey is a Professor of Media at Ball State University where he also serves as the Director of Graduate Studies. His previous books include *Hollywood Gamers, Digital Convergence in the Film and Video Game Industries*, and *Playing to Win: Sports, Video Games, and the Culture of Play*. His work has appeared in *Games and Culture* and *Convergence*.

Jason Phillips is a Lecturer in the Media department at Ball State University. His previous academic work has focused on music videos, gender in the media, and internet culture. He has also worked professionally in broadcast journalism. He is a member of Gen-X, so he's well-versed in both *Star Wars* and Marvel, though he prefers DC and thinks the prequel *Star Wars* films were actually pretty good.

Timothy Pollard is Associate Dean Emeritus for Academic Affairs and Student Relations in the College of Communication, Information, and Media at Ball State University. He held the position from 2019 to his retirement in 2022. He provided managerial oversight for academic programs, supported faculty development, and ensured positive student relations in the college. Mr. Pollard has been with Ball State since 1998 and, prior to his elevation to Associate Dean, served in the Department of Telecommunications as an Associate Professor and chair from 2011 to 2017. Previously, he worked for CNN in Atlanta and Washington, D.C.

Routledge Research in Cultural and Media Studies

Celebrity and New Media
Gatekeeping Success
Stephanie Patrick

Mediatisation of Emotional Life
Edited by Katarzyna Kopecka-Piech and Mateusz Sobiech

Serial Killers in Contemporary Television
Familiar Monsters in Post-9/11 Culture
Edited by Brett A.B. Robinson and Christine Daigle

The Eurovision Song Contest as a Cultural Phenomenon
From Concert Halls to the Halls of Academia
Edited by Adam Dubin, Dean Vuletic and Antonio Obregón

Drag in the Global Digital Public Sphere
Queer Visibility, Online Discourse and Political Change
Edited by Niall Brennan and David Gudelunas

Crowds, Community and Contagion in Contemporary Britain
Sarah Lowndes

Global South Discourse in East Asian Media Studies
Dal Yong Jin

Bias, Belief, and Conviction in an Age of Fake Facts
Edited by Anke Finger and Manuela Wagner

Reasserting the Disney Brand in the Streaming Era
A Critical Examination of Disney+
Robert Alan Brookey, Jason Phillips and Timothy Pollard

For more information about this series, please visit: https://www.routledge.com

Reasserting the Disney Brand in the Streaming Era

A Critical Examination of Disney+

Robert Alan Brookey, Jason Phillips and Timothy Pollard

Routledge
Taylor & Francis Group
LONDON AND NEW YORK

First published 2023
by Routledge
4 Park Square, Milton Park, Abingdon, Oxon OX14 4RN

and by Routledge
605 Third Avenue, New York, NY 10158

Routledge is an imprint of the Taylor & Francis Group, an informa business

British Library Cataloguing-in-Publication Data
A catalogue record for this book is available from the British Library

ISBN: 978-1-032-42235-0 (hbk)
ISBN: 978-1-032-42867-3 (pbk)
ISBN: 978-1-003-36465-8 (ebk)

DOI: 10.4324/9781003364658

Typeset in Sabon
by codeMantra

Contents

1 Sign In or Sign Up

Disneyland has only shut down three times since it opened in 1955. The first shutdown occurred following the assignation of John F. Kennedy, and the second shutdown followed the terrorist attacks on 9/11 (Knowles, 2020). The park was again shut down in March 2020 due to the COVID pandemic. This final closure was significantly longer, as the park remained closed until California eased health restrictions and allowed Disneyland to reopen in April 2021. In important ways, these closures index these crises and locate the pandemic in relation to other historical events in the US. COVID, however, was not a crisis specific to the US, but was a global pandemic and over several months, shutdowns and lockdowns were an international experience. Many industries were affected, and many layoffs and business closures followed, as the pandemic proved to be both a health crisis and an economic one.

The impact of the pandemic on the media industries was radical. Worldwide lockdowns forced people indoors for inordinate amounts of time. Closures of movie theaters, concert venues, and sporting arenas forced many (if not most) people to find entertainment options in their own homes (Fortmueller, 2021). Fortunately, streaming services provided these people with more options, offering subscribers new original programming and the chance to binge-watch old favorites. Throughout the pandemic, the viewing habits of people changed as more streaming options became available. Subsequently, subscriptions to these services increased 26% according to a report from the Motion Picture Association, estimating that total streaming subscribers topped 1 billion (Faughnder, 2021). Several services were already in place, with others in various stages of development. For many media companies, these services would be their primary mode of connecting with audiences. Disney is a case in point. In addition to the closure of Disneyland, their other theme parks around the globe were closed at one time or another, their cruise ships were docked, and their live theater performances were shut down along with the cinemas. Given that the parks also functioned as important retail outlets for Disney's ancillary products, the company had few revenue streams remaining, and one of those was very new and yet untested: Disney+.

DOI: 10.4324/9781003364658-1

Disney+ was the company's entry into what has been called the "streaming wars," a rather hackneyed metaphor used to reference the competition these services faced in attracting viewers and subscribers. Admittedly, there were several streaming, or Over-The-Top (OTT), services already in place before the pandemic, including Netflix, Hulu, Amazon Prime Video, and CBS All Access (rebranded as Paramount+). Prior to the lockdowns, two new services were launched, including Disney+ and Apple TV+ which both premiered in November 2019. During the early months of the pandemic, other high-profile services would be launched including Peacock from NBCUniversal (Comcast) and HBO Max from WarnerMedia (later Warner Bros./Discovery). These services were high-profile because they were tied to legacy media brands, but were designed to transition these brands for the streaming market. Like Disney, these companies would use these services to introduce new content, repurpose their back catalogs of films and television programing, and augment or replace the theatrical release of their films. Yet, at the risk of stating the obvious, none of those services carried the Disney brand. As Mart Ots has noted, "Media brands offer value propositions about what their customers can expect in terms of types of content, interactivity, and user experience" (2008, p. 3). Indeed, Disney is a brand that has signaled family-friendly content to media consumers for several decades. To that end, it has also been very successful: according to Interbrand, a marketing consultancy that ranks global brands across all market segments, Disney is 10th on their list of the Best Global Brands of 2021 (InterBrand, 2022).

Sylvia Chan-Olmsted (2011) has observed that the multi-channel media market, and the rise of social media, presents both challenges and opportunities to scholars studying media branding. She argues for an "OPEN" media brand studies that focus on four basic topics: "on-demand, personal, engaging and networked" (2011, p. 8). Although she is not referencing streaming services specifically, all four of these topics apply to streaming services generally. Chan-Olmsted offers a brief example of the challenges of streaming services when she observes that a CBS show streaming on Hulu could become disassociated from its network brand. Where Disney+ is concerned, however, the challenge was not brand disassociation, but rather the close association of the various brands the company owned.

While the launch of Disney+ was important to the company as a means of connecting with consumers and maintaining a source of revenue during the pandemic, we should also note the service was not designed with a health crisis in mind. Instead, the service was designed to compete with other streaming services, and clearly Disney was using its own brand, and the brands of the companies it has acquired over the years, to meet this competition. For proof, one need not look further than the service itself. The Disney+ interface features sections clearly identified by the labels Pixar, Marvel, Star Wars, and National Geographic. While other services (like Netflix) may organize content by genre, Disney+ orders its content by brand.

Under those labels, subscribers found legacy content mixed in with new Disney+ original content produced specifically for the service. These brands have been acquired over the years as Disney bought out Pixar, Marvel, Lucasfilm, and 21th Century Fox, and arguably Disney+ is literally a product (if not the culmination) of these acquisitions. Although Pixar, Marvel, and Star Wars films may have featured the Disney logo in the opening credits, seldom have all of these brands been so closely and visibly associated within the same media consumer product, and seldom has Disney's supremacy as the parent company brand been so obvious.

While the Disney+ interface is designed to associate these brands, these brands signify a vast amount of content, much of which reflect narratives and characters that are in several respects different from the worlds imagined by Disney. There was little Disney could do to alter this legacy content, particularly for those brands that have established audiences, without alienating some of the fans that make up those audiences.[1] The original content created for the Disney+ service, however, was another matter entirely. That content could be created to reflect the Disney brand, while still appealing to the audiences that are attracted by Pixar, Marvel, Star Wars, and National Geographic content.

Disney+ presents an important opportunity to examine the company and it various brands at a rare moment in the media environment. Granted, Disney, as a company, has received extensive scrutiny, particularly from academics, but many of these studies engaged a very different and much smaller company than the one that exists today. For example, the anthology *From Mouse to Mermaid*, a collection of critical essays, was published before Disney had even acquired ABC (American Broadcasting Company)/CapCities (Bell, Haas & Sells, 1995). In *The Disneyization of Society*, Alan Bryman (2004) describes how the practices within Disney's theme parks are incorporated into various businesses. While Disney provides the template for Bryman's analysis, he engages Disney before the acquisitions of the brands that would make up Disney+, and his critical attention is devoted to companies other than Disney. In their book *The Mouse that Roared*, Henry A. Giroux and Grace Pollock (2010) raise significant concerns regarding the continued media consolidation that had allowed Disney to grow into a conglomerate with holdings across a variety of mediums and a global reach. While they acknowledge both the acquisition of Pixar and Marvel, they devote little time to the significance of those acquisitions, and their book predates the acquisition of Lucasfilm and Fox.

In the recently updated edition of *Understanding Disney*, Janet Wasko (2020) refreshes her comprehensive discussion of Disney and discusses the various mergers and acquisitions made by Disney. She casts many of these acquisitions as the outcome of various boardroom machinations and essential personalities in the Disney story as it evolved from the 1990s on. She also notes an emphasis on corporate synergy and branding and the expansion of the Disney brand in relation to its acquisitions. While she discusses the history of those acquisitions, she does not engage the content that has emerged after the acquisitions occurred, or the way those acquired brands have been strategically exploited through Disney+. It should be noted that this edition was made available (at least on Amazon) on January 20, 2020, only two months after the launch of Disney+. Therefore, it is unlikely that Wasko had access to Disney+ while preparing the manuscript. Our purpose is to pick up where Wasko left off and provide a focused engagement of Disney+, its brands, and its content.

This book is intended to do just that. We do not offer it in contrast to the work just mentioned, but as an extension, to reconsider Disney now that it has become a much larger company and one that has faced some of the most significant challenges to the entertainment industry. We intend to analyze Disney's acquisition of Pixar, Marvel, Lucasfilm, and Fox, but we will do so through a critical lens focused on the Disney+ service. Specifically, in the chapters that follow, we will look at how Disney has used these acquisitions to launch the service and then critique the original content that they have produced for the service. In this chapter, we lay the groundwork for those analyses. First, we trace the emergence of streaming services and discuss the various services that make up Disney's competition in this market. We then provide a critical history of Disney in which we trace the practices that former CEO Bob Iger identified as preparing the company for the streaming wars, back through the leadership regimes of Walt Disney and Michael Eisner. Finally, we will discuss the theoretical and methodological rationale for our study and provide a preview of the chapters that follow.

From VCR to Streaming

Although streaming services represent a relatively new technology, we should note that these services need to be understood in relationship to some older technologies. For example, the VCR or video cassette recorder. Although video tape had been around for several years, and the older reel-to-reel video tape players were used by the industry (and in some educational contexts), they never had a viable consumer market. The VCR, and video cassettes, were considered much more user-friendly, and ushered in a new form of media consumption: the home video market. The first VCR was the Sony Betamax, introduced in 1975, but it soon met competition with the JVC VHS format which was released in 1976. For various reasons (Cusumano, Mylonadis & Rosenbloom, 1992), the VHS format took hold in the consumer market. This market was a revolutionary change for the media industries, as it created a secondary market primarily for film, but also for some popular television shows. It also ushered in new consumer practices, such as video rentals, and provided consumers with expanded home entertainment options.

The VCR formats, however, were analog recordings which were limited in both their quality and functionality. The cassettes contained magnetic tape that would be dragged across the tape heads of the players, creating a consumer experience that was decidedly linear and occasionally interrupted by audio and video problems due to the physical erosion of the tapes. The introduction of the DVD in 1997 was another technological revolution. DVDs contained digital files read on discs using lasers, and they offered a better consumer experience in both video and audio quality, one that was more dynamic and interactive than video tape.[2] In addition to the traditional functions of fast-forward and rewind, consumers could skip to specific scenes using the interactive menus of the DVDs. They could also enjoy a variety of extra features not often offered on video tape, including audio commentaries, behind the scenes segments, deleted scenes, and interviews. All of these features were also immediately accessible through the DVD interface. Therefore, the DVD introduced even more options for consumers than the old VHS format; it also changed the home video market from a rental market to a sell-through one, meaning that instead of renting consumers were buying DVDs (Rothman, 2004). Although rental giants like Blockbuster and Hollywood video transitioned to offering DVD rentals, consumer decisions to buy instead of rent significantly eroded the market. Yet the real threat the DVD format posed to the rental market was its place in the emergence of subscription services, or more specifically, Netflix.

Netflix is a classic Silicon Valley story from the late 1990s, involving two entrepreneurs, Marc Randolph and Reed Hastings. Randolph and Hastings came up with the idea for a DVD-by-mail sales and rental system, based on the assumption that DVDs (unlike VHS tapes which had several breakable plastic parts) could be easily shipped through the mail with minimal damage. The first DVD they shipped was sent to Hastings' house, and it arrived unscathed. From this successful experiment, they started to build the company. On April 14, 1998, Netflix launched the first online DVD rental store with 30 employees and 925 titles, encompassing almost the entire stock of DVDs in print at the time (Netflix Inc., n.d.). As consumers began embracing DVD technology, and as the players and discs became cheaper, Netflix's subscription base started to increase as well (McCord, 2014). Starting in late 1999, the start-up disrupted the rental market significantly since it eliminated the late fees charged by brick-and-mortar rental stores (Silva, 2020). Instead, consumers would pay a monthly fee, for which they could view as many DVDs as they like, but they could only have three titles at any given time. Still consumers enjoyed the relative convenience of Netflix, which allowed them to return titles in a postage-paid envelope through the mail, all for a set subscription fee. Although the DVD technology facilitated the emergence of Netflix, the company was well aware that another technological advancement was on the horizon.

By the mid-2000s, high-speed internet service delivered the bandwidth and data speed that made video streaming relatively seamless, without the buffering and glitches on slower services. Netflix began considering online delivery options, including a proposed "Netflix Box" that would download movies overnight, so that they could be watched the next day. This idea was scrapped, but in January of 2007, the company introduced its streaming service (Rodriguez, 2017). Although Netflix was not the first to offer digital video online (Apple was offering downloads of television shows as early as 2005), it has become the dominant force in the video streaming market, and although it has started to lose subscribers, it still has 220 million subscribers worldwide (Goldsmith, 2022). Netflix, however, was not the first streaming service offered to consumers, because that honor is held by Amazon.

Amazon began offering online video downloads in 2006 under the "Amazon Unbox" label (Statz, 2006). Since then, Amazon's video services would go through several different iterations including "Amazon Video on Demand," "Amazon Instant Video" before becoming "Prime Video" (Boas, 2018; Downey, 2018). Unlike Netflix, for which subscriptions are its primary revenue stream, Amazon Prime Video is offered as just one of many amenities enjoyed by Amazon Prime customers. That is not to say that Amazon does not take video content seriously in its business model. Indeed, they have entered the original content game and have enjoyed some critical success. In 2014 Amazon had its first legitimate hit, *Transparent*, which garnered critical acclaim over its four-season run, and has received numerous awards (Bahr, 2019). From then on, Amazon has had its fair share of hits (and misses) like any streaming platform. Most recently, however, *The Marvelous Mrs. Maisel* (2017) has emerged as one of the service's signature series garnering numerous Primetime Emmys and Screen Actors Guild awards.

In a move that also is indicative of Amazon's commitment to content for its streaming service, the company acquired MGM in May 2021. Granted, the iconic film studio had certainly declined over the years and had changed ownership several times. Yet, as Dade Hayes (2021) has observed, Amazon is looking to integrate MGM's historic film catalog into its Prime Video service. Although that integration will be delayed by the various streaming deals that MGM has already established with other services, the $8.5 billion deal (the second largest acquisition in the company's history) signifies a strong commitment to Amazon's Prime Video service.

Shortly after Netflix and Amazon began offering streaming content, Hulu was officially launched on March 12, 2008. It was created by a variety of investors and partners including, NBCUniversal (owned by Comcast), News Corporation (parent of the Fox Broadcasting Company and 21st Century Fox), Yahoo!, AOL, and Facebook (Lamare, 2018). The Disney Company purchased an equity stake in Hulu on April 30, 2009, and it would start to provide some of its library of television shows and movies through the service, significantly expanding Hulu's offerings (Moore, 2019). When Disney acquired Fox, the deal included Fox's percentage stake in Hulu. As a result, Disney became the majority owner of Hulu (Gold & Riley, 2017). Another equity partner, AT&T (owner of WarnerMedia), sold its nearly 10% stake back to Hulu so that it could start its own streaming service, HBO Max. Finally, on May 14, 2019, Comcast gave Hulu control to Disney, although Comcast's stake will not be sold to Disney until 2024. This move allowed NBCUniversal to launch its own streaming service, Peacock (more on that later).

With Disney now in charge of Hulu, it has started to package Disney+, Hulu, and ESPN+ for one fee. As with any streaming service, content is king. The strategy to bundle these services offers various Disney-owned properties to the consumer. With Hulu, Disney can now stream any content that does not fit under the Disney+ label, including R-rated films, and is doing so with some of the content it has acquired from Fox. For example, the Hulu service contains a section specific to the offerings from the FX cable network, which was acquired in the merger. The FX network (which includes FXX and FXM) is branded as "fearless," and much of its programing, including the drag ball show *Pose*, reveals the type of content that Disney is able to offer on Hulu, while reserving Disney+ for content more readily associated with the parent brand.[3]

If anything, the control of Hulu allows Disney to further curate the content it places on the Disney+ service. This curative function was displayed when the service decided to forgo the planned *Lizzie McGuire* reboot because of its adult themes. It also moved a series spinoff of the film *Love, Simon* (2018), entitled *Love, Victor* (2020), to Hulu because of its gay themes (Chavez, 2020). In addition, Hulu has also offered content from the brands that appear on the Disney+ service that would not set comfortably under the Disney brand. For example, *Hit Monkey* is an animated series that premiered on Hulu in 2021. The series is based on a relatively obscure Marvel character, and in the opening scene of the series the simian assassin brutally murders several men in a bloody, albeit animated, massacre. *Hit Monkey* is the Marvel exception that proves the rule regarding the branding practices that have informed the content on Disney+.

Indeed, Disney's strategic use of both Disney+ and Hulu as packaged platforms allows it to offer a variety of content aimed at a variety of audiences, while still protecting the Disney brand. Disney needed this strategic edge as it was launching into an already competitive market (given the dominance of Netflix), a competition other companies were eager to enter, including those from other industries. For example, Apple.

Although Apple TV had been around in various iterations (as both hardware and software), its Apple TV+ service was launched about the same time as Disney+, in November 2019. This launch also signified the company's first foray into original content. The critical consensus on that content has been mixed at best, although the service has enjoyed some success with Ted Lasso (2020–2021) (Trenholm, 2019). Apple CEO Tim Cook has also brushed off the option of picking up the kind of deep libraries of content that have benefitted Netflix and Hulu (Leswing, 2020) in the form of such series as *Friends* (1994), *Seinfeld* (1989), and *South Park* (1997). It seems that Apple is committed to an alternative approach to the streaming business, a philosophy perhaps consistent with its corporate persona.

WarnerMedia, on the other hand, is a company with a long history in media production, which can be traced back to the early years of the film industry. When the company announced the launch of its streaming service, HBO Max, in late 2018, they made it clear they would use their extensive and historic library to attract paid subscribers and thereby pivot from the cable/satellite systems that birthed HBO. The streaming service mirrored the competition by aggressively pushing new content (along with a catalog of popular HBO shows) onto its service to entice more people to subscribe. The zeal to increase subscribers, along with the COVID-19 pandemic, helped push management to put the entire slate of 2021WarnerMedia films on the streaming service. This announcement shocked traditional Hollywood, who were aghast at the approach. CEO John Stankey stated that the decision was made with the customers in mind and that AT&T would "adjust and work the model differently" if and when audiences returned to the theaters once the pandemic comes to an end (Sherman, 2020).

In May of 2021, AT&T announced plans to merge WarnerMedia with Discovery, a company which holds among its cable brands HGTV, OWN, and TLC. The merger is designed to better position the combined company in the global market for streaming services. In June 2021, it was announced that the future company will be called "Warner Bros. Discovery," with a tagline taken from the 1941 Warner Bros. film *The Maltese Falcon*: "the stuff that dreams are made of." Unfortunately, the announcement was met with derision, as many people tweeted comments suggesting the new name is decidedly unimaginative (Spangler, 2021). As rebranding goes, not an auspicious beginning. In fact, issues of branding became more complex when new Warner Bros. Discovery CEO David Zaslav announced that the Discovery+ streaming service will be merged into HBO Max. One service is associated with award winning content, while the other offers reality television; clearly different brands. Although he did not disclose the name of this combined service (the shorten "Max" was being considered), or which brand it would embrace, Zaslav did indicate that his company is considering offering an ad-supported option for the service (Arkin, 2022).

NBCUniversal, on the other hand, drew on the iconic NBC logo when naming its Peacock streaming service, which it officially launched on July 15, 2020; its internet and cable customers received early access to the service in April (Webb, 2020). One of the big reasons Peacock launched during this time was to showcase the 2020 Tokyo summer Olympics. However, due to COVID, the sporting event was postponed. Even without the "tent pole" of the Olympics to help drive subscribers, Peacock still launched. The built-in library from NBC and Universal Pictures allows the streaming service to hit the ground running, providing customers with opportunities to binge-watch their favorite NBC shows, such as *Will and Grace* (1998) and *The Office* (2005). The Universal library gives subscribers the *Fast and*

Furious (2001) series and classics such as Alfred Hitchcock's *Psycho* (1960) and *Rear Window* (1954). As of July 2022, it had an estimated 28 million active accounts, but only 13 million of those were paid subscriptions. Peacock is a service that is free to Comcast customers, and to those that chose an ad-supported option of the service. Although those ad-supported accounts still generate advertising revenue, Peacock still has lost Comcast $467 million (Forristal, 2022).

Unlike WarnerMedia (or rather, Warner Bros. Discovery), NBCUniversal (and parent company Comcast) ended up with a more balanced approach to the theatrical market. In April of 2020, NBCUniversal used the release of *Trolls World Tour* (2020) to test the strategy of releasing a film to the theatrical market while simultaneously making the film available through the Comcast OnDemand cable service for an additional fee (or premium video on demand, or PVOD). This strategy was not well received by the AMC theater chain, which threatened to cancel the exhibition of future Universal films. However, the two companies would reach an agreement providing a 17-day exclusive window for Universal films to appear in AMC theaters before becoming available through PVOD. The deal allows Comcast to offer these films through their OnDemand cable service, but surprisingly not through their Peacock streaming service (Lee, 2020). In ways, this deal indicates that Comcast is using a multi-platform approach similar to Disney's, but one that is designed to make their legacy cable service still seem attractive to consumers while establishing a footprint in the market that may render that cable service obsolete.

Viacom, by way of contrast, entered the streaming services market well ahead of these other legacy media conglomerates when it launched CBS All Access in October 2014. This service offered exclusive content, some of it spun off of its more popular shows; for example, *The Good Fight* (2017) features characters from the hit show *The Good Wife* (2009). In 2020, ViacomCBS CEO, Bob Bakish, announced that CBS All Access would change its name to Paramount+ in early 2021, with an emphasis on live sports, breaking news, and a "mountain of entertainment" (Escandon, 2020). The official launch occurred on March 4, 2021, and Paramount+ promised to become a repository of content from the ViacomCBS libraries that would grow the service over the years to compete with the other streaming services. By 2021, Paramount+ had 43.3 million paid subscribers (Spangler, 2022). To put that into perspective, Disney+ is reported to have attracted 95 million subscribers in a little over a year; it took Paramount+ (and CBS All Access) eight years to generate half the subscribers that Disney+ generated in about one (Spangler, 2021).

Although the "Streaming Wars" is an overwrought metaphor, it signifies the fact that all of these services are looking to attract subscribers. As consumers decide how many and which services they will choose, there will be winner and losers. For example, Quibi, the short-form video content service headed by former Disney executive Jeffery Katzenberg and Meg

Whitman, was launched in April 2020, but was closed before the year was out; clearly a loser. Disney+, however, appears to be a winner. The data analytics company Apptopia (2021) reported that Disney was second only to Netflix among downloaded video entertainment applications for the first three quarters of 2021, however it generated the most gross revenue of any service (including Netflix) during that same period. While this might seem counter-intuitive given Netflix larger subscriber base, Disney generated additional revenue by charging a premium for theatrical films and special events released on the service, *Black Widow* and *Hamilton*, for example.

This success, however, has not come without some set-backs; subscriber growth has significantly slowed for the service (Strange, 2021), and there have been reports of conflicts arising in the transition from Bob Iger to Bob Chapek as Disney CEO (Masters, 2021). These conflicts were early indications that Chapek was not well suited for the position, and ultimately he would be removed and, in a remarkable move, Iger would be brought back as his replacement. In spite of these corporate machinations, Disney+ is still a service to be reckoned with; for example, Zaslav has identified Disney+ as one of the prime competitors for his company's own streaming service. In addition, Kris Naudus (2021), writing for *Engadget*, argues that Disney+ is one of the most important services to be launched, because of its strategic use of the company's media franchises.

We agree. The success Disney+ has enjoyed is due to the way the company has deployed its various media brands. For example, the service has drawn on the company's Marvel Cinematic Universe (MCU), with such shows as *WandaVision* (2021) and *Loki* (2021). *The Mandalorian* (2019), an original series situated in the Star Wars universe, was a massive hit for Disney+ and resulted in an increase in subscriptions (Gartenberg, 2021). In addition, Pixar and National Geographic also offer attractive content, along with the variety of Disney films and television shows available on the service. In other words, the success of the service can be attributed not only to consumer loyalty to the Disney brand, but also loyalty to the other media brands that define the structure of the service and make up its content. The success of this brand strategy is perhaps best indicated in 2022 when Disney+ bested Netflix; it reported 221 million subscribers in the third quarter, compared to Netflix 220 million (Goldsmith, 2022). Therefore, Disney and Disney+ provide a case worthy of consideration and further investigation, particularly regarding media brands and their importance to the survival of legacy media in this transition to streaming services. We believe this for a couple of reasons.

First, and at the risk of stating the obvious, it is Disney. As we have noted earlier, Disney is one of the most recognized media brands. We mentioned the Interbrand rankings earlier, and although Interbrand ranks both Apple and Amazon over Disney (ranking them first, and second, respectively), both the Apple and Amazon brands are known globally as purveyors of good and services other than entertainment media. Disney's presence on this list, however, is due to their entertainment content offerings, and all other goods and services are tied to those offerings. Netflix, on the other hand, as a brand wholly constituted by the streaming and production of entertainment content, is arguably more closely related to Disney than either Apple or Amazon. Yet, Netflix is only ranked as 36th on Interbrand's list. Therefore, Disney has always been a more recognized brand than Netflix. As Fortmueller (2021) has observed, Disney+ has proven to be the only service that is competing with Netflix on a global level. Studying the Disney+, and its deployment of brand in this new market gives us insight into how the company navigated this challenging new media market.

Second, it appears for the moment that Disney is actually beating Netflix in the streaming market, where the total number of subscribers in concerned. Granted, given the problem of "churn" in the streaming market (subscribers continually dropping and adding services), Disney's slim 1 million subscriber lead over Netflix could change. Still, Disney is clearly a force to be reckoned with. This is especially true given that the existing scholarship on streaming services has been focused on Netflix.

For example, in *From Networks to Netflix* (2018), Derek Johnson and a host of contributors cut a wide swath across the television and streaming landscape to examine a plethora of changes to the industry in a streaming era. The book covers more than Netflix (Hulu and Amazon, for example) and it also takes a deep dive by examining the impact of streaming on such niche markets as adult/pornographic programming via Playboy TV and professional wrestling/sports entertainment through an analysis of the surprisingly disruptive WWE Network. Yet the book predates the emergence of Disney+. So too is the case for *The Netflix Effect* (2016), edited by Kevin McDonald and Daniel Smith-Rowsey. Its chapters focus on everything from Netflix's programming strategies, to textual analysis of shows, to building audiences, to defining (and redefining) genre. Indeed, with its heavy focus on Netflix, any discussion of Disney typically mentions it as one of several major media conglomerates in various contexts.

Mareike Jenner's (2018) *Netflix and the Re-invention of Television* does mention the importance of Hulu to establishing a legitimate and official means of accessing a variety of entertainment programing not offered on Netflix, but this is before Disney bought out Fox and acquired control of the service. Catherine Johnson (2019) in *Online TV,* discusses the launch of a Disney SVOD service in the UK called Disney Life, but of course that service has been eclipsed by Disney+. Amanda Lotz's book *Netflix and Streaming Video* (2022) was published in time to engage the Disney+ service, but her engagement of Disney+ seems dismissive. While she acknowledges that Disney+ is more similar to Netflix than Amazon Prime Video or Apple TV+, she posits "adding Disney+ may be like buying a bike when you already have a car" (Netflix) (2022, p. 112). The recent subscription numbers seem to indicate that people, as they often do in real life, have no trouble owning a bike and a car, and some may have decided they can get by with just "bike."

Therefore, we set out in the book to engage both Disney and Disney+ in order to understand how this legacy media company successfully entered the streaming market. Yet, in order to properly position Disney in the contemporary context, we need some historical context. In the section that follows, we will provide a history of Disney leadership in order to explain how the company's past strategies seemed to have secured its future. We structure this brief history to focus on the leadership regimes of Walt Disney, Michael Eisner, and Bob Iger. More specifically, we take the business strategies that Iger has identified as important to the launch of Disney+, and the future of the company, and show how those strategies have historically informed the practices of the company and its leadership. Or more to the point, our analysis shows how Disney's entry into the streaming market was in many respects, business as usual.

A Decidedly Specific History of Disney

One of the first spokespersons for the Disney+ streaming service was, of all people (or characters), Bart Simpson. In a commercial for the service, Bart appears in a Mickey Mouse costume protesting, "I'm not going to do it. You're not going to make me do it. I don't care how much they pay." Homer, wearing an Iron Man costume, threatens: "You put on those nose and ears or I'm going to take off yours." Bart complies, and the rest of the Simpson family, wearing costumes culled from Disney and Star Wars films, pose while Homer orders: "Now everybody smile!" Clearly, the commercial draws on the irony of Bart Simpson now being a form of intellectual property wholly owned by Disney, following Disney's acquisition of Fox on March 20, 2019. In fact, Bart's contrarian attitude, and his general resistance to authority, anchors the humor of the commercial; and for the record, Disney paid over $71 billion for Fox and Bart.

According to then Disney CEO Robert Iger, it was Rupert Murdoch who approached Disney with the possibility of buying Fox. As Iger notes, Murdoch saw how big tech companies were moving into media production and distribution, and he did not believe his own company was large enough to weather the challenges that lay ahead. Disney, Murdoch thought, could handle those challenges. As Iger notes, with the acquisition of Fox, "Disney would be facing the future in a stronger position than it had ever been in" (Iger, 2019, p. 205). Still, Iger also noted that the acquisition presented challenges:

> We couldn't just add them to what already existed; we had to integrate them carefully in order to preserve and create value. So, I asked myself: What would, could, or should the new company look like? If I were to erase history and build something totally new today, with all of these assets, how would it be structured?
>
> (Iger, 2019, p. 209)

Iger then outlines the strategies that he believes should guide the "new" Disney: content, technology, physical entertainment, and consumer products. Later, he observes how these strategies mirror the strategies he presented to the Disney board in 2004 when he was being considered as a replacement to former CEO Michael Eisner: "making high-quality branded content, investing in technology, and growing globally" (Iger, 2019, p. 219). In addition to Fox, Iger also oversaw the acquisition of Pixar, Marvel, and Lucasfilm (and the Star Wars franchise). By some estimates, Iger has quadrupled Disney's market capitalizations with these acquisitions (Berkowitz, 2020).

Although Iger claims that to prepare Disney for the streaming wars, he had to "erase history and build something totally new," the strategies he defines are hardly new to the company (Iger, 2019, p. 209). Since the time of Walt Disney[4] himself, the Disney Company has been involved in the cultivation of content, the exploration of technology, and the globalization of the company brand through its theme parks and products. In this section, we trace those practices through the leadership of Walt Disney, Michael Eisner, and Bob Iger. These three have been the most visible leaders of the company, and it has been argued that the company floundered under other leadership regimes (Stewart, 2006). While we use these leaders as markers for the emergence of these practices, our focus is more on the practices than the people. We also want to pivot from the word "strategies" to the word "practices" because we want to break from any assumptions about a purposeful, linear progression. Instead, we want to acknowledge that while these practices have facilitated the launch of Disney+, they certainly predated any planning for the service, conceptually or otherwise. Finally, ours is not a traditional historical analysis, as we will not be drawing on primary sources. As Kung (2006) has noted, when it comes to corporate leaders as primary sources, they are often inaccessible and not always forthcoming or honest about company practices; and in the case of our study, one of the primary sources is dead. Instead, we will draw on biographies, news stories, and industry analyses to trace practices through three periods that we call "The Walt Disney Era," "The Michael Eisner Era," and "The Bob Iger Era."

The Walt Disney Era

Walt Disney's animation career began in Kansas City, but in 1923 he decided to move to Hollywood to make it big. Like many who made this move before him (and after), Walt first struggled to find employment and recognition as an animator. After some qualified success with the *Alice Comedies* (1923–1927) series, which combined animation and live-action footage, he landed a contract with Universal to produce the *Oswald the Lucky Rabbit* (1927) cartoons. The contract was negotiated with Disney's distributor, Charles Mintz, but Walt Disney's charge was rather vague: Universal Studios wanted a cartoon about a rabbit. Walt and his fledgling animation team created the character of Oswald, and the cartoon series proved popular with audiences and critics. Yet, when it came time to negotiate the contract for the next series of Oswald cartoons, Mintz dropped his price from $2,250 per cartoon to $1,800. When Walt balked at this significant drop in compensation, Mintz threatened to take both the animation studio and the series away from him. Walt soon learned that most of the members of his animation team had already committed to Mintz and that Universal owned the intellectual property rights to Oswald (Thomas, 1994). In other words, Mintz was already set to move forward with the production of more Oswald cartoons without Walt Disney's involvement.

It was a humiliating loss for Walt Disney, particularly given that he had to work with his disloyal animation team to finish his commitment to the Oswald series. Yet, simultaneously and surreptitiously, Walt was working on a cartoon entitled *Plane Crazy* (1928), which featured his new creation, Mickey Mouse. Unfortunately, *Plane Crazy* failed to find a distributor. However, when Mickey Mouse later appeared in the sound production cartoon *Steamboat Willie*, released in 1928, a cultural icon was born (Thomas, 1994).

Walt Disney learned an essential lesson from this experience: intellectual property ownership is necessary for artistic control. Even prior to the character being pried from Walt Disney's budding portfolio, Universal had changed the nature of the character and the tone of the animated films involving the character. Walt Disney did not just lose the character in a business transaction. Rather, he arguably lost it bit by bit, film by film, change by change. Disney as a company seems self-aware that its signature control over (and often micromanagement of) intellectual property is a direct legacy of Oswald the Rabbit (Thomas, 1994).

Walt Disney would also learn that intellectual property was a valuable commodity. Mickey Mouse began to move merchandise shortly after *Steamboat Willie* appeared in theaters. The Ingersoll Company produced its first Mickey Mouse watch in 1933 (Thomas, 1994). Indeed, Disney was a pioneer in licensing and distributing ancillary products, and those practices have been expanded and accelerated over the years. Walt Disney also instituted a philosophy of control and standardization with respect to licensing, merchandising, and intellectual property (Anderson, 1994). This provided a variety of benefits to his company, ranging from successful marketing strategies, to ensuring product quality, to developing a consistent brand identity among target audiences. More than 50 years after his passing, the Walt Disney Company is still committed to developing and exploiting intellectual property, and any visit to a Disney park reveals how much space is devoted to the retailing of the resulting ancillary products. As Douglas Gomery (1994) has noted, this merchandising, distribution and branding has helped the company to survive during some lean times in its early days.

Despite the humiliation associated with the Oswald incident, the relationship between Walt Disney and Universal gave the fledgling animation company a serious boost of cash. Timothy Susanin and Diane Disney Miller (2011) outline the ventures made possible because of the money made off of Oswald. Chief among those – acquisition of land, investment in the development of animation techniques, increased staff, and more money to stabilize the company in various ways. As such, losing control of Oswald set the company on its current course in many ways because controlling the intellectual property is a primary practice at Disney and certainly informs the company's acquisitions. One acquisition seems to have flown under the radar and arguably functions more as an effort to return Disney to its roots. In 2006, Disney acquired the rights to the cartoon character Oswald the Rabbit from NBCUniversal in a trade that oddly involved sportscaster Al Michaels, a longtime staple of Disney-owned ABC's *Monday Night Football* (1970). While the wheeling and dealing with Michaels had as much to do with the particulars of the sports broadcasting business as anything (Goldman, 2011), the Oswald-for-Al trade does demonstrate, ultimately, where Disney's priorities lie in the 21st century.

In addition to his rightful place in animation history, Walt Disney was also a pioneer in television, although he waited until the right strategic moment to fully engage the then-new technological medium (Wasko, 2001). While other film studios cast a jaundiced eye toward television technology, Walt Disney saw a ripe opportunity to diversify his media offerings. Walt certainly was open to new media and new entertainment technologies, even if they challenged current business practices. In a 1953 *Variety* guest column, Walt obliquely referenced his vision of how TV could be a catalyst to support and promote the Disney brand to the masses (Gray, 2020). Indeed, he would use television to introduce the Disney parks, pioneer youth-oriented programming with *The Mickey Mouse Club* (1955), and promote new films and repurpose famous scenes from the old ones with *The Wonderful World of Disney* (1954). As Walt noted, the entertainment industry "calls for constant adaptation and adventures in showmanship. . . Ours has long been a chance-taking business" (Gray, 2020, para. 4).

In this case, the "chance-taking" paid off. The financial success of Disney's early investment in television ventures also meant more money in the company's coffers – a recurring theme in the Disney story. As the 1960s began, the company had the resources to develop its live-action film business. As such, Disney's ventures into television were not just about the company expanding into a new medium. Rather, and perhaps more importantly, they were about diversifying the content so that Disney was no longer just an animation studio.

Walt Disney clearly understood television's value in promoting other elements of his burgeoning empire (Jackson, 1993). Walt Disney executed this practice in various ways, some involved the repurposing of Disney films and cartoons and some involved using television as a promotional vehicle for Disney projects in the pipeline. Most notably, *The Disneyland Show*, which premiered in 1954, provided updates on the development of the Disneyland theme park, identified the "lands" and narratives the park would be based around, and gave viewers a look behind the scenes at the technology of the parks' various rides and exhibits (Cotter, 1997). In order to design the park, Disney formed WED Enterprises in 1953, an engineering and architectural division that was tasked with developing the technologies for both Disneyland and Disney World. These technologies would often be on display during segments of the show, providing heightened anticipation for viewers and their children. By the time the parks opened, viewers not only knew plenty about them, but also had been introduced to the technology behind the scenes.

It is a fairly common observation to frame Walt Disney's entry into the theme park business as a mixture of personal will (family trips to other amusement parks inspired him), corporate drama (a lot of roadblocks, literal and figurative, popped up along the way), and a realization of the need for brand expansion (to connect Disney fans with experiences outside the home and the cinema). But putting buildings on land is a much more expensive proposition than even making films or cartoons. As such, Walt Disney needed the one thing that perhaps the Oswald the Rabbit debacle has conditioned him to be wary of – partners.

The Disneyland Show (1954) launched as part of a deal with ABC that involved the network contributing financially to the theme park project (Stewart, 2006). Specifically, the Walt Disney Company, Walt Disney himself, ABC (which also owned Paramount Theatres at that time), and Western Publishing all had various stakes in the project. As we have noted, the television partnership, in particular, proved fruitful on a variety of fronts. Also, the ABC money went a long way toward financing the project, and perhaps more importantly, from a long-term perspective, the seeds of Disney's ultimate ownership of ABC were sown here. But Disney never seemed interested in partnerships with other independently owned entities, so he soon gained control of the theme park that bore his name and for whom he was the primary spokesman.

Although Disneyland opened in Anaheim in 1955, by 1960, the Disney corporation had acquired all of ABC's shares and secured complete ownership of Disneyland (Kubersky, 2017). Considering that Walt Disney conceived the project in the late 1940s (Glover, 2013), it took less time for Walt Disney to acquire complete ownership of the company than it did to build it. Clearly, he was not interested in having a partner for any longer than necessary. Still, the opening of Disneyland, and his preliminary planning and execution of Disney World, set the stage for the primary practices that Iger identifies as strategies for the "new" Disney.

In the Walt Disney Era, we see the emergence of three core business practices. First, Disney cultivated content by branching out into television and used the parks as an extension of the narratives and themes of the film and television content. This cultivation was in no small part augmented by Walt Disney's commitment to the ownership and control of the intellectual property. Second, his early start in television can also be seen as a commitment to technological advancement, at a time when television sets were considered a new consumer technology. In addition, Walt Disney incorporated the use and expansion of technological developments to deliver different experiences in the parks. Third, there is the introduction and use of the theme parks as spaces for the exploitation of intellectual property through retailing, but just as important, the parks would serve as a launching point for the globalization of the Disney brand, particularly under Eisner. Although the globalization efforts seem slight during the Walt Disney Era, he made one deal that would set up one of the company's first international expansions. In 1959, Walt Disney licensed the use of his studio's characters to appear on playing cards produced by Nintendo for the Japanese market.

The Michael Eisner Era

Before coming to Disney in 1984, Eisner had worked at ABC and then became the President at Paramount when Barry Diller hired him in 1976. While at Paramount, Eisner oversaw the production of several films that were not only hits but became part of the popular culture zeitgeist at the time, including *Saturday Night Fever* (1977), *Flashdance* (1983), and *48 Hrs.* (1982). Eisner first joined Disney as the CEO and as part of a team that would include Frank Wells as president and Jeffery Katzenberg as chairman of Walt Disney Studios. In 1994, Wells would die in a helicopter crash, and Eisner would replace him as president. Eisner then fired Katzenberg, which would set off one of the most contentious lawsuits in the industry at the time. Arguably this firing would be Eisner's first significant misstep (Masters, 2014), but for our purposes, we will focus on Eisner's accomplishments that reflect a continuation of certain practices.

The first changes that occurred under Eisner must, of course, also be attributed to Frank Wells. They both took tours of Disneyland and Disney World and began changing the way these parks figured into the mix of the company's business practices. The hours at Disneyland were expanded, and the park began a 365-day operating schedule in 1985. Advertising for Disneyland was significantly expanded, so the park was now marketed nationally rather than just locally. In addition, Eisner and Wells established teams representing the different operational divisions within the parks that, in turn, would facilitate communication across the parks (Stewart, 2006). The purpose of these teams was to establish and share best practices across all of Disney's parks at the time. This level of attention is notable for two reasons. First, it stood in sharp contrast to the relative negligence of the parks under the previous, post-Walt Disney leadership. Second, it signified an understanding of how integral the parks could become to Disney's business practices moving forward. When Eisner was questioned about the poor performance of some Disney films, he countered by pointing out how vital the other revenue streams were to the company's overall health

(Stewart, 2006). The parks figured heavily in that revenue mix because they generated income from attendance fees, hotel and resort charges, and food and concessions. And as we have noted earlier, the parks also provided prime retail space for the numerous ancillary products spun off Disney's media products.

Although the older management regime would be responsible for the opening of Tokyo Disneyland, the park had only been in operation for about a year when Eisner joined Disney. Although the park is owned and operated by a Japanese company (The Oriental Land Company), Disney receives licensing fees for its intellectual property in the form of percentages on admissions, food and beverage, and ancillary product sales (Raz, 1999). Disney, however, does provide some management support in employee training, and clearly, Eisner had a significant role in overseeing the park in its early years, particularly in order to protect and project the Disney brand. He was often the corporate voice for the park, mainly when it came to US business press coverage (Van Maanen, 1992). Under his leadership, Tokyo Disneyland rose to become one of Disney's most popular and successful parks.

Disneyland Paris (called initially Euro Disney) would be Eisner's project from the ground up. Although several locations in Europe were considered for the park, the final location near Paris was favored by Eisner (Stewart, 2006). While Eisner felt the location would elevate Disney in its association with French culture, the French had a decidedly different view of this association. Politicians, journalists, and intellectuals spoke out against the park and regarded Disney as a threat to French culture specifically and European culture generally (Renaut, 2011). Perhaps because of this resistance, the park would open in 1992 to less than spectacular results. Euro Disney would be plagued with various problems over the years, and through most of its history, has continued to record losses (Storey, 2017). Although Disneyland Paris could be considered one of Eisner's failures, it was part of his efforts to increase corporate commitment to the parks, and both Hong Kong Disneyland and Shanghai Disney Resort would also begin under his tenure.

Although Hong Kong Disneyland has proven to be much more successful than Paris Disneyland, it too often operates at a loss (Cheng, 2018). Shanghai Disneyland opened in 2016, and although initial ticket sales were strong, attendance has been inconsistent. Despite these problems, Eisner's commitment has been carried forward; Disney completed a buyout of Paris Disneyland in 2017, and Iger publicly announced Disney's commitment to the Shanghai park in 2018. We should note that Eisner's efforts to expand the parks also functioned to expand Disney's global presence while drawing on the various technologies the company developed for the rides and attractions. Eisner was responsible for changing WED Enterprises into Walt Disney Imagineering. He also oversaw an expansion of this division into new facilities, including sound stages and production offices in 1997.

Under Walt Disney's guidance, the studio had a very clear and single focus on its content production: family-friendly entertainment. As we have noted, however, Walt Disney did begin expanding and diversifying Disney's media products. Eisner, however, was instrumental in expanding Disney's content production outside of the family entertainment market, and he did so under the Touchstone Pictures label. Although Touchstone was already in place at Disney before Eisner's arrival, and had scored a hit with *Splash* (1984), under Eisner the imprint would release *Down and Out in Beverly Hills* (1986), *Ruthless People* (1986), *The Color of Money* (1986), *Three Men and a Baby* (1987), *Good Morning Vietnam* (1987), *Who Framed Roger Rabbit* (1988), *Pretty Woman* (1990), *Sister Act* (1992), *What's Love Got to Do with It* (1993), and *Nightmare Before Christmas* (1993). To put that output into perspective, Touchstone released films chronicling a group of deceitful con artists, films romanticizing a prostitute and a pool-shark, and a biopic depicting the violent abuse inflicted on Tina Turner by her husband and musical partner Ike Turner. Hardly film fare one would expect from Disney. In addition, Touchstone released two animated features that significantly departed from Disney's typical offerings: *Who Framed Roger Rabbit* and *Nightmare Before Christmas*, although Disney would fully embrace the latter film once it became a classic (Brookey, 2010).

This departure into more adult-oriented content was very successful for Disney, as many of the titles listed above would not only prove to be box office hits, but also become iconic films of the late 1980s and early 1990s. In other words, under Eisner, Disney began to produce, market, and distribute a much more diverse portfolio of content. This diversification would be significantly expanded when Eisner acquired Miramax in 1993. Miramax, a film distribution and production company founded by Bob and Harvey Weinstein, specialized in independent and foreign films.[5] Many of these films, some directed by Gus Van Sant and Quentin Tarantino, would prove to be even more outré than those released by Touchstone. In fact, the controversial content of Miramax films inspired a boycott by the Catholic Church and the Southern Baptist Convention; religious organizations that claimed Disney had abandoned family values (Donohue, 1995).

This diversification through acquisition would continue under Eisner when he moved to acquire Cap Cities/ABC. Capital Cities had begun in the 1940s as Hudson Valley Broadcasting Company, but it had grown over the years through acquisitions of radio stations, television stations, newspapers, and magazine publishers. The company would acquire ABC in 1985, and the merged conglomerate would become Cap Cities/ABC. When Disney purchased the company in 1996 and the legacy broadcast network, they also received the cable holdings, which included the A & E networks, Lifetime, and most notably, ESPN. At the time, the $20 billion deal was one of the largest in US history, and it would double the size of Disney as a company (Stewart, 2006). Having begun his career at ABC, Eisner was able to make a convincing case that he was well-positioned to take on this new responsibility.

Several media companies were combining operations to maximize shareholder value and get content out to multiple outlets during this period. In many ways, this foreshadowed the current consolidation of assets for streaming. TimeWarner merged with Turner Broadcasting, and CBS merged with Westinghouse and then was purchased by Viacom. With the acquisition of Cap Cities/ABC, Disney became a model of the emerging media conglomerate, with holdings in film, television, music, publishing, and theme parks. When synergy was the new buzzword in the industry, Disney was often held up as the exemplar of a company that could exploit content across a broad range of distribution windows (Wolf, 1999). In addition, Disney had holdings across a wide swath of entertainment media that crossed all genres and media divisions.

Eisner was also instrumental in establishing a relationship with Pixar, releasing the first feature-length computer-animated film. This relationship would prove to be very fruitful for Disney but would ultimately lead to Eisner's downfall. The multiple-picture deal that Pixar cut with Disney split costs and revenues, but because Disney retained a distribution fee on Pixar's films, Disney made more money off Pixar films than Pixar did. After the success of *Finding Nemo* (2003), Steve Jobs, who owned the computer animation company, wanted a better deal, and when Eisner balked, Jobs began negotiating with other studios on a distribution deal for Pixar's future films. Unfortunately for Eisner, this conflict with Jobs came when Disney's animation offerings failed to score at the box office. In addition, Eisner had overseen a significant cut in Disney animation, closing several studios and laying off several animators. Roy Disney, who oversaw Disney animation, was already angry over the cuts Eisner had made to animation. When the conflicts with Jobs arose, Roy Disney mounted a "Save Disney" campaign to rally shareholders against Eisner (Powers & Brookey, 2005). The campaign worked, and Eisner resigned as Disney CEO and stepped down from the Disney board in 2005.

Under Eisner, however, we can see the continuation and expansion of the three core business practices previously outlined. Content expanded significantly under Eisner, with the increased success of Touchstone and the acquisitions of ABC and Miramax. The collaborations with Pixar would signify both the emergence of a new animation technology and an additional source of content. Eisner also significantly expanded the theme parks and created footprints for the Disney brand in the Asian and European markets, thereby expanding the company's global reach. He created, or at least renamed, the Imagineering program and opened new facilities to develop new technologies. In other words, these three core business practices were already in place when Iger began his term as CEO.

The Bob Iger Era

Like Eisner, Robert (Bob) Iger began his professional career at ABC. He moved up the ranks, and in 1989 was named head of ABC Entertainment.

In 1993, he moved to the president's chair of the ABC Network Television Group, and in 1994 he took the reins as president and CEO of Capital Cities/ABC. Iger survived the merger with Disney, but in 1999 Eisner named him president of Walt Disney International and moved him up to chairman of the ABC Group. His unit oversaw all of the company's international operations and Iger "expanded and coordinated Disney's presence outside of the United States, establishing the blueprint for the Company's international growth today" (Robert A. Iger, n.d.). In 2000, Bob Iger was named president and chief operating officer (COO) of The Walt Disney Company. This was the first time that Michael Eisner named a COO for the company after the tragic death of its previous COO, Frank Wells, in 1994. After the "Save Disney" campaigned successfully removed Eisner, Iger took over as CEO, and his tenure at Disney has, without a doubt, ushered in significant changes for the company.

Primarily these changes were brought about by the acquisitions that Iger oversaw. His first purchase was Pixar in 2006 for $7.4 billion. It was a natural fit since Pixar's brain trust of John Lasseter, Brad Bird, Pete Docter, and others were graduates of the CalArts animation program that Walt Disney founded. In addition, Steve Jobs was the largest shareholder in Pixar, and he and Iger were on the same page about growing animation. Once the purchase was complete, Jobs became Disney's largest stakeholder. With Disney's business and marketing expertise, Pixar could grow and flourish. Roy Disney gave his blessing by stating:

> Animation has always been the heart and soul of The Walt Disney Company, and it is wonderful to see Bob Iger and the company embrace that heritage by bringing the outstanding animation talent of the Pixar team back into the fold. This clearly solidifies The Walt Disney Company's position as the dominant leader in motion picture animation, and we applaud and support Bob Iger's vision.
>
> (Greenfield, 2011, para. 4)

In 2009, Iger's team purchased Marvel Entertainment for $4 billion. In return for that investment, the MCU has sold more than $20 billion in tickets worldwide, excluding merchandising (Quitoriano, 2019). This acquisition was followed by the 2012 merger with Lucasfilm for $4 billion. Although there was a lot of concern about George Lucas selling to Disney, it has paid off with the resurgence in *Star Wars* movies and its spinoffs. In that same year, Bob Iger was also named chairman of Disney, as well as continuing as CEO.

Iger's biggest acquisition occurred in 2019 when Disney bought several assets from Fox. This purchase included the 20th Century Fox film and television studios, additional Marvel characters (including the X-Men and Deadpool), controlling interest in Hulu, several US cable and satellite channels, and Indian broadcaster Star India. This purchase gives Disney 40% of the US moviemaking market along with unprecedented marketing and branding opportunities. The Star India purchase gives the company a foothold in one of the largest global media markets.

Clearly, the acquisitions made by Iger have significantly diversified the media content owned by Disney. However, many of these acquisitions should also be viewed from the perspective of intellectual property. Indeed, Lucasfilm and Marvel are both companies that have already fully exploited the ancillary market before being purchased by Disney; in fact, Marvel Studios was created out of a desire to sell action figures and toys (Brookey, 2010). Therefore, these were not just acquisitions of companies; they were, in effect, the accumulation (and cultivation) of intellectual properties. The MCU is a case in point. Since the Disney acquisition in 2009, Marvel has released over 20 films, even allowing for the Spider-Man films produced by Sony, which comes to about two films released each year. Each of those releases was accompanied by attendant releases of branded ancillary products. In other words, these acquisitions increased content production and created new opportunities for consumer products.

In addition, under Iger, these acquisitions have been fully integrated into the theme parks. Disney World opened the Star Wars: Galaxy's Edge attraction in August of 2019 (although COVID-19 soon shut it down). Iger's purchase of Lucasfilm allowed Disney to cement a relationship that was already in place in the parks: the *Star Wars* based Star Tours ride was opened at Disneyland in 1987, and later in Disney World and Tokyo Disneyland. In addition, the Indiana Jones Adventure ride was opened in Disneyland 1995, and the Indiana Jones Temple of Peril ride was opened in Disneyland Paris in 1993. Disneyland Paris has opened a newly renovated Hotel New York – The Art of Marvel, with public spaces and rooms decorated with characters from the Marvel universe. Under Iger, *Toy Story* Land sections have been opened in Paris Disneyland, Hong Kong Disneyland, Shanghai Disneyland, and Disney World. Also, under Iger, the Pandora section of Animal Kingdom opened in 2017, as if in anticipation of the Fox merger (the 2009 blockbuster *Avatar* was acquired with Fox). These new attractions also featured the work of the Imagineers, using technology to bring these narrative worlds to life. Finally, although the planning of the Hong Kong and Shanghai parks began under Eisner, Iger has been primarily responsible for the opening and operation of those parks. Therefore, it is clear that the attention to the theme parks did not waiver under his regimen.

Of course, the launch of Disney+ is perhaps the best example of Iger's emphasis on technology. One of Iger's acquisitions that did not receive as much attention as the others was that of BAMTech. In 2016, Iger acquired a 33% share of the streaming video company and then bought controlling interest in 2017 from Major League Baseball, which owned the service (Spangler, 2017). Iger would use this service as the core technology for Disney+ and even changed the name of the company to Disney Streaming Services in 2019. In his biography, Iger (2019) points to the launch of Disney+ as one of the company's most essential and important commitments to technology.

In February 2020, Iger announced his intention to step down as Disney CEO and named his successor – Bob Chapek. In a matter of weeks, however, the COVID pandemic shut down a good deal of Disney's businesses. In April of 2020, it was announced that Iger would retain control of the business operations, and it was later announced that he would continue to do so throughout 2021 (Goldsmith, 2021). We will revisit this somewhat rocky transition in corporate leadership in the sixth chapter. Where Iger's tenure is concerned, however, he followed through on the very practices that he identified as necessary. Yet, as we have demonstrated in this section, those practices (the cultivation of content, the expansion of technology, and the globalization of the company brand through parks and products) did not begin under Iger. Instead, those practices can be traced back through the tenure of Eisner to the birth of the company under Disney. That is not to say that Iger has not been an exemplary steward of the Disney brand. Undoubtedly, he took those practices and expanded the company in extraordinary ways. Yet, Iger inherited a legacy on which he could build the company into what it is today. In other words, the "new" Disney is not all that different from the old one. In spite of all the acquisitions that Iger made, he was adding to a company that had an established identity and a very valuable brand. Indeed, the Disney+ service reveals how its various brands have been contained under the Disney label, and we would argue that the original content created for the service from these various brands (Pixar, Marvel, Star Wars, and National Geographic) reflects the type of content associated with Disney. Indeed, it appears the practices that prepared Disney+ to enter the streaming market we already in place. Actually, that will be the point that we will stress throughout the book: in spite of all the talk about streaming services disrupting the media industry, the launch of Disney+ reveals a company relatively undisrupted. In fact, in our analysis of the original content on the service, we find programing that not only reflects the core traits of the Disney brand, but we show how the production of this content reflects established Disney business practices.

Disney Undisrupted

In the chapters that follow, we will critique the original content made available when the Disney+ service launched, content that appeared under Pixar, Marvel, Star Wars, and National Geographic labels. Our choices were informed by the visibility this content received on the service interface at the time of the launch. Since that launch, some of our choices have proven to be more popular than others, but the content we chose to critique was prominently positioned to promote the service. Our purpose is to identify the textual elements of this content to reveal how Disney has maintained these brands and executed them with the launch of Disney+. We conduct a critical, textual analysis of this content, grounding those analyses in the context of the acquisitions that Disney has made, and in some cases, the historical conditions of Disney's productions, and in other cases, challenges that the company was facing in relation to those brands. Our intent is to better understand how this content not only helped launch the service, but also served the interests of Disney as a company generally. The individual chapters will call on different theoretical constructs in order to engage the texts, but there is some broader theoretical work that we would like to consider that encompasses all of the chapters.

We anchor our critical project in the study of media political economy. This study has a long history that can be traced back to the work of Horkhiemer and Adorno (1972) and their critique of the cultural industries. More specifically, we approach our study under the assumption that corporate interests are manifest in media content, even entertainment content (Mosco, 2009). The literature regarding the political economy of the media is quite broad, and even a representative review is beyond the scope of our project. We do, however, see important touchstones in the literature that inform our analysis.

For example, Joseph Turow (1997) has identified and critiqued the synergistic practices of media conglomerates, and Disney+ reveals these practices in action. However, while Turow mentions the repurposing of content, what we see with Disney+ is creating new content that often draws on the intellectual property that Disney has acquired; in other words, a repurposing of intellectual property. Ronald V. Bettig (1996) identified the importance of intellectual property 25 years ago when he discussed the value of repurposing older media content for new media distribution systems, and he identifies Disney as a case in point, and Disney+ is clearly an effort to extend that value. Other important work that informs our study includes Derek Johnson's (2013) investigation of media franchises as Disney+ draws on these franchises for content and uses their brands to organize the interface.

The literature on branding that we discussed earlier was posited for empirical applications, but we should note that there is essential work that looks at media branding from a critical perspective. In his book *Brand Hollywood: Selling Entertainment in a Global Media Age*, Paul Grange (2008) provides an extensive review of the literature on media branding. For the sake of brevity, we will not reproduce that review here. We should note, however, that Grange purposefully sets Disney to one side for his analysis. This choice is understandable because the Disney brand had already been heavily scrutinized. He wanted to investigate how branding operated (and proved problematic) for other media conglomerates. Jennifer Gillan's (2015) book *Television Brandcasting: The Return of the Content Promotion Hybrid* devotes an entire chapter to a variety of Disney branded content and cross-promotion. In ways, our work extends Gillan's to engage the other media brands that Disney owns, and to show how those brands were deployed with the launch of Disney+.

In our critiques of Disney+ original content, we will draw on a framework of the "Classic Disney" style. Wasko (2001) synthesizes several studies of the Disney brand into a simple framework that includes elements of style, story, characters, themes, and values. More specifically, in terms of style, Wasko identifies light entertainment, music, and humor. In terms of story, she identifies "revised fairy tales or folklore" and the "classic Hollywood cinema model" (2001, p. 114). As for characters, they include "anthropomorphized, neoterized animal characters, formulaic heroines, heroes, villains and sidekicks, stereotypical representations of gender and ethnicity" (2001, p. 114). The themes and values Wasko identify include individualism, optimism, innocence, and the triumph of good over evil. This framework will provide the general critical lens through which we will view the texts in our analyses. We will remark on the elements that reflect this framework and consider other theoretical perspectives that we believe are relevant to the specific texts and contexts.

For example, the second chapter is devoted to Pixar. In ways, the integration of Pixar into Disney was relatively painless, as all of Pixar's films have been in collaboration with Disney. In addition, Disney had a significant influence on Pixar as it developed as an animation company. For example, John Lasseter, who joined Pixar in 1983 and would produce Pixar's early films, including *Toy Story* (1995), *A Bug's Life* (1998), and *Cars* (2006), was trained in animation by Disney artists when he was a student at the Disney supported CalArts. He was hired by Pixar after he had been fired from Disney and would return to the company as Chief Creative Officer of Walt Disney Animation Studio after the merger. Lasseter took a leave of absence in 2017 following allegations of sexual misconduct. He has not returned to Disney, and instead joined Skydance animation studios as CEO. The conditions of his departure can be contextualized as part of the #MeToo movement that exposed and challenged the rampant sexism in the entertainment industries (Masters, 2017). In this chapter, we will focus our attention on *Purl* (2018), a short Pixar film that not only appeared on Disney+ at its launch but was also used to promote the service prior to the launch. In the manner of the Classic Disney style, the film posits an overly optimistic and easy resolution to the problem of workplace sexism. Our analysis locates *Purl* in relation to Lasseter's tenure at Disney and Pixar and his ultimate departure. We maintain that *Purl* is both oversimplistic in its resolution of workplace sexism and highly problematic given the conditions that Lasseter created at Pixar.

For the chapter on Marvel, we focus on *Marvel's Hero* Project (2019), a reality show that rewards the efforts of young people who have committed themselves to help others. These young people are reimagined as Marvel superhero characters, and Marvel produces comic books that illustrate their stories. In addition, each of the young people featured receives a Marvel jacket and $10,000 for their chosen charities. While this is a nice honor, and each of these young people is treated with great respect by the show, we point out that Marvel (and Disney) now owns the rights to the stories and new individuals' likeness as rendered in the comic. In other words, it turns these young people into intellectual property, property Disney has acquired at minimal cost. In this chapter, we compare both the text and the production context of *Marvel's Hero Project* to Disney's iconic *The Mickey Mouse Club*. We argue that Disney reproduces elements of that old show in the production of the new one, and it also reproduces its practices of extracting high value at minimal costs from the young people involved.

In the chapter on Lucasfilm, we show how the merger with Disney is a logical outcome of over 40 years of synchronicity between the two companies. We also discuss the history of the *Star Wars* franchise and how George Lucas fell out of favor with some of the most ardent fans of this franchise. We consider this content in our analysis of the Disney+ series *The Mandalorian* (2019) and show how the series reflects the elements of the Classic Disney style, and does so in a way that reflects practices of fan service. In this chapter, we depart from our methodological choice of limiting our analyses to content that launched with the Disney+ service. On May 4, 2020, Disney+ offered a new series *Disney Gallery: The Mandalorian*. This series provided a behind-the-scenes perspective on the making of *The Mandalorian*, and we include an analysis of this additional paratext. We do so because this paratextual series is directly and inextricably linked to the original Disney+ series. In addition, *Disney Gallery: The Mandalorian* addresses the fan discontent with George Lucas, albeit indirectly, and attempts to appease those fan concerns while also incorporating practices of fan service.

When the merger with Fox was completed, Disney would receive the 20th Century Fox productions studio, its film vault, Fox Searchlight Pictures, and television networks, such as FX and National Geographic. As we mentioned in the preface, Disney is already repurposing much of the content they received in this acquisition on Hulu. And while *The Simpsons* (1989) resided on Disney+, it is National Geographic that enjoys its own category on the service. We focus our analysis on the Disney+ original program *The World According to Jeff Goldblum* (2019). This show explores several subjects and objects, some that are rather mundane (bikes, jeans, and sneakers, for example), and imbues them with historical and intercultural depth. We analyze the show from the perspective of banal cosmopolitanism and argue that while the show seems to offer a broader understanding of the significance of these subjects and objects, that understand firmly holds to the Classic Disney style. More to the point, while Goldblum does identify some problematic issues in his explorations, those problems are quickly dismissed. In other words, *The World According to Jeff Goldblum* offers us a world that is ultimately wonderful.

In the concluding chapter, we return to the problems of the pandemic and the status of Disney during the COVID-19 crisis. Although all film studios experienced a significant drop in revenue while theaters were closed, Disney experienced additional losses from the closure of their parks and the suspension of their cruises and live theater offerings. We argue that Disney+, therefore, became an essential service in which customers could engage with the Disney brand and experience. In fact, we contend that while the parks were closed, the streaming service functioned as a virtual theme park, allowing guests to move from one narrative space to another at their will and leisure. The parks have long been recognized as remediation of the narratives contained in Disney's films. This remediation has been augmented by the digital interfaces through which guests have experienced the park, either through the webpage or the mobile apps. We maintain that Disney+ becomes a remediation of the theme park experience, bringing that experience and the stories they convey home quite literally. Yet, we maintain that the similarities between the Disney parks and Disney+ are not limited to the remediation of content. Instead, we argue that just as Disney has instituted surveillance practices in the parks, similar surveillance happens on the service as viewers' movements are tracked as data points. In this way, the Disney+ service, like the parks themselves, render up data about Disney consumers that is then used to extract more value from these customers. Again, our analysis will reveal how the content the service draws from Disney's established business practices and serves the company's interests. While our investigation ends at the parks, we begin with Pixar.

Notes

1 The controversy surrounding George Lucas, and the negative reaction of fans to the changes he made to his own films, is a case in point. In fact, an entire documentary entitled *The People vs. George Lucas* was released in 2010, chronicling the disdain fans felt toward Lucas, and we explore this controversy in greater detail in Chapter 4.

2 The Laser Disc was a precursor technology for the DVD, although this earlier format did not enjoy a large consumer market base.

3 We should note that this curation of content is not universal as Hulu is not a service available international. In other countries Hulu content is offered on the Disney+ service. For example, as one of us observed in a trip to Spain, the Hulu original *Only Murders in the Building* (2021–2022) appears and is promoted on Disney+.

4 For our purposes when we refer to the person, we will use his full name: Walt Disney. When referencing the company, we will use the name: Disney.

5 We revisit this acquisition in the next chapter. Harvey Weinstein's convicting of rape was part of the larger #MeToo movement that would lead to John Lasseter's departure from Pixar.

References

Anderson, C. (1994). *Hollywood TV: The studio system in the fifties.* Austin: University of Texas Press.

Apptopia. (2021). Benchmarking the streaming video entertainment landscape. *Apptopia.* Retrieved from https://engage.apptopia.com/hubfs/2021%20Streaming%20Landscape%20Report/Apptopia%202021%20Streaming%20Landscape.pdf

Arkin, D. (2022, August 4). HBO Max and Discovery+ will combine into single streaming service. *NBC News*. Retrieved from https://www.nbcnews.com/business/business-news/hbo-max-discovery-will-combine-single-streaming-service-rcna41551

Bahr, R. (2019, September 15). 'Transparent: musical finale': TV review. *The Hollywood Reporter*. Retrieved from https://www.hollywoodreporter.com/review/transparent-musicale-finale-review-1239775

Bell, E., Haas, L., & Sells, L. (1995). *From mouse to mermaid: The politics of film, gender, and culture*. Bloomington: Indiana University Press.

Berkowitz, J. (2020, February 27). How Bob Iger's Disney changed the entertainment industry forever-for better and worse. *Fast Company*. Retrieved from https://www.fastcompany.com/90468643/how-bob-igers-disney-changed-the-entertainment-industry-forever-for-better-and-worse

Bettig, R. (1996). *Copyrighting culture: The political economy of intellectual property*. Boulder, CO: Westview Press.

Boas, M. (2018, March 14). The forgotten history of Amazon video. *Medium*. Retrieved from https://medium.com/@mikeboas/the-forgotten-history-of-amazon-video-c030cba8cf29

Brookey, R. (2010). *Hollywood gamers: Digital convergence in the film and video game industries*. Bloomington: Indiana University Press.

Bryman, A. (2004). *The Disneyization of society*. Thousand Oaks, CA: Sage Publishers.

Chan-Olmsted, S. (2011). Media branding in a changing world: Challenges and opportunities 2.0. *The International Journal of Media Management*, *13*(1), 3–19.

Chavez, N. (2020, February 29). Hilary Duff says 'Lizzie McGuire' revival can't be 'real and relatable' if it has to be PG. *CNN*. Retrieved from https://www.cnn.com/2020/02/29/entertainment/hilary-duff-lizzie-mcguire-reboot-trnd/index.html

Cheng, K. (2018, February 20). Gov't-backed Hong Kong Disneyland see net loss of HK$345 million in 2017- third year in the red. *Hong Kong Free Press*. Retrieved from https://www.hongkongfp.com/2018/02/20/govt-backed-hong-kong-disneyland-sees-net-loss-hk345-million-2017-third-year-red/

Cotter, B. (1997). *The wonderful world of Disney television: A complete history*. New York: Hyperion.

Cusumano, M., Mylonadis, Y., & Rosenbloom, R. (1992). Strategic maneuvering and mass-market dynamics: The triumph of VHS over Beta. *Business History Review*, *66*, 51–94.

Donohue, W. (1995, May 26). Something stinks in the Magic Kingdom: "Priest."' *Catholic League for Religious and Civil Rights*. Retrieved from https://www.catholicleague.org/something-stinks-in-the-magic-kingdom-priest/

Downey, R. (2018, February 8). Amazon Prime video name change has one purpose. *The Streaming Advisor*. Retrieved from https://thestreamingadvisor.com/amazons-prime-video-name-change-has-one-purpose/

Escandon, R. (2020, November 13). Paramount+ on track to replace CBS all access next year. *Forbes*. Retrieved from https://www.forbes.com/sites/rosaescandon/2020/11/13/paramount-on-track-to-replace-cbs-all-access-next-year/?sh=4e4387e915c6

Faughnder, R. (2021, March 18). Streaming milestone: Global subscriptions passed 1 billion last year. *Los Angeles Times*. Retrieved from https://www.latimes.com/

entertainment-arts/business/story/2021–03–18/streaming-milestone-global-subscriptions-passed-1-billion-last-year-mpa-theme-report

Forristal, L. (2022, July 22). Peacock's paid subscribers stayed flat at 13 million, losses widen to $467 million. *TechCrunch*. Retrieved from: https://techcrunch.com/2022/07/28/peacocks-paid-subscribers-stayed-flat-at-13-million-losses-widen-to-467-million/

Fortmueller, K. (2021). *Hollywood shutdown: Production, distribution, and exhibition in the time of COVID*. Austin: University of Texas Press.

Gartenberg, C. (2021, February 11). Disney Plus hits 94.9 million subscribers, beating its four year goal in 14 months. *The Verge*. Retrieved from https://www.theverge.com/2021/2/11/22278874/disney-plus-94–9-million-subscribers-q1–2021-earnings

Gillan, J. (2015). *Television brandcasting: The return of the content promotion hybrid*. New York: Routledge.

Giroux, H., & Pollack, G. (2010). *The mouse that roared*. Lanham, MD: Rowman & Littlefield.

Glover, E. (2013, August 30). This week in Disney history: Document outlining early concept for Disneyland is shared, 1948. *Disney Parks*. Retrieved from https://disneyparks.disney.go.com/blog/2013/08/this-week-in-disney-history-document-outlining-early-concept-for-disneyland-is-shared-1948/

Gold, H., & Riley, C. (2017, December 14). Disney is buying most of 21st Century Fox for $52.4 billion. *CNN*. Retrieved from https://money.cnn.com/2017/12/14/media/disney-fox-deal/index.html

Goldman, L. (2011, August 19). 47 years in the life of Al Michaels. *Business Insider*. Retrieved from https://www.businessinsider.com/al-michaels-2011-8

Goldsmith, J. (2021, March 9). Bob Iger bids Disney shareholders farewell at his last annual meeting. *Deadline*. Retrieved from https://deadline.com/2021/03/disney-bob-iger-annual-shareholders-meeting-1234710204/

Goldsmith, J. (2022, August 11). Disney's streaming services just passed Netflix in total subscribers. *Deadline*. Retrieved from https://deadline.com/2022/08/disney-just-passed-netflix-in-total-streaming-subscribers-1235089361/

Gomery, S. (1994). Disney's business history: A reinterpretation. In Smoodin, E. (Ed.), *Disney discourse* (pp. 71–86). New York: Routledge.

Grange, P. (2008). *Brand Hollywood. Selling entertainment in a global media age*. New York: Routledge.

Gray, T. (2020, December 21). Walt Disney's 1953 Variety guest column: 'We must compete as never before.' *Variety*. Retrieved from https://variety.com/2020/film/news/walt-disney-guest-column-1953-1234853321/

Greenfield, R. (2011, October 7). Disney CEO Robert Iger will step down in 2015. *The Atlantic*. Retrieved from https://www.theatlantic.com/business/archive/2011/10/disney-ceo-robert-

Hayes, D. (2021, May 26). MGM will plug into Amazon streaming machine as it hits higher gear. *Deadline*. Retrieved from https://deadline.com/2021/05/mgm-amazon-streaming-machine-prime-video-fire-tv-1234764738/

Horkhiemer, M. & Adorno, T. (1972). *Dialectic of enlightenment*. New York: Herder & Herder.

Iger, B. (2019). *The ride of a lifetime: Lessons learned from 15 years as CEO of the Walt Disney Company*. New York: Random House.

InterBrand. (2022). Best global brands 2021 rankings. *Interbrand*. Retrieved from https://interbrand.com/best-global-brands/

Jackson, K. (1993). *Walt Disney: A bio-bibliography*. Westport, CN: Greenwood Press.

Jenner, M. (2018). *Netflix and the re-invention of television*. Cham, CH: Palgrave MacMillan.

Johnson, C. (2019). *Online TV*. New York: Routledge.

Johnson, D. (2013). *Media franchising: Creative license and the collaboration in the culture industries*. New York: NYU Press.

Johnson, D. (Ed.) (2018). *From networks to Netflix: A guide to changing channels*. New York: Routledge.

Knowles, H. (2020, March 13). Disneyland closing for third time in history as major theme parks shutter in response to coronavirus. *The Washington Post*. Retrieved from https://www.washingtonpost.com/travel/2020/03/12/disney-is-closing-its-california-theme-parks-coronavirus-precaution/

Kubersky, S. (2017, February 12). Who owns the Disney parks around the world? *Attractions Magazine*. Retrieved from https://attractionsmagazine.com/owns-disney-parks-around-world/

Kung, L. (2006). Preface. In Kung, L. (Ed.), *Leadership in the media industry* (pp. 5–7). Jönkoping, Sweden: JIBS Research Report Series.

Lamare, A. (2018, July 31). How streaming started: YouTube, Netflix and Hulu's quick ascent. *B2: The Business of Business*. Retrieved from https://www.businessofbusiness.com/articles/a-brief-history-of-video-streaming-by-the-numbers/

Lee, C. (2020, July 29). What AMC and Universal's historic streaming deal really means for moviegoers. *Vulture*. Retrieved from https://www.vulture.com/2020/07/amc-and-universals-historic-streaming-deal-explained.html

Leswing, K. (2020, February 26). Cook says Apple TV+ is focused on original programming *CNBC*. Retrieved from https://www.cnbc.com/2020/02/26/apple-shareholder-meeting-cook-talks-apple-tv-health-acquisitions.html

Lotz, A. (2022). *Netflix and streaming video*. Medford, MA: Polity Press.

Masters, K. (2014, April 9). The epic Disney blow-up of 1994: Eisner, Katzen and Ovitz 20 years later. *The Hollywood Reporter*. Retrieved from https://www.hollywoodreporter.com/features/epic-disney-blow-up-1994-694476

Masters, K. (2017, November 21). John Lasseter's pattern of misconduct detailed by Disney/Pixar insiders. *The Hollywood Reporter*. Retrieved from https://www.hollywoodreporter.com/news/john-lasseters-pattern-alleged-misconduct-detailed-by-disney-pixar-insiders-1059594

Masters, K. (2021, October 6). Bob Iger's long goodbye. *The Hollywood Reporter*. Retrieved from https://www.hollywoodreporter.com/business/business-news/bob-iger-disney-exit-bob-chapek-succession-1235025504/

McCord, P. (2014, January 1). How Netflix reinvented HR. *Harvard Business Review*. Retrieved from https://hbr.org/2014/01/how-netflix-reinvented-hr

McDonald, K. & Smith-Rowsey, D. (Eds.). (n.d.). *The Netflix effect: Technology and entertainment in the 21st Century*. New York: Bloomsbury.

Moore, C. (2019). Hulu and the 5 things that set it apart from other streaming giants. *Fox Business*. Retrieved from https://www.foxbusiness.com/technology/5-things-to-know-about-hulu

Mosco, V. (2009). *The political economy of communication*. London: Sage.

Naudus, K. (2021, November 12). In just two years, Disney+ has become one of the most important streaming services. *Engadget*. Retrieved from https://www.engadget.com/disney-plus-day-state-of-the-union-173020959.html

Netflix, Inc. History. (n.d.). *Funding Universe*. Retrieved from http://www.fundinguniverse.com/company-histories/netflix-inc-history/

Ots, M. (2008). Media brands: New ground to explore. In Ots, M. (Ed.), *Media brands and branding* (pp. 1–7). Jönköping, SE: Jönköping International Business School.

Powers, A., & Brookey, R. (2005). Michael Eisner was framed: Newspaper narrative of corporate conflict. In Picard, R. (Ed.), *Corporate governance of media companies* (pp. 183–202). Jönkoping, Sweden: JIBA Research Report Series.

Quitoriano, George G. (2019, April 28). How much money has the MCU franchise made in total? *Quora*. Retrieved from https://www.quora.com/How-much-money-has-the-MCU-franchise-made-in-total

Raz, A. (1999). The hybridization of organizational culture in Tokyo Disneyland. *Culture and Organization, 5*(2), 235–264.

Renaut, C. (2011). Disneyland Paris: A clash of cultures. In Jackson, K.M., & West, M.I. (Eds.), *Disneyland and culture: Essays on the parks and their influence* (pp. 125–137). Jefferson, NC: MacFarland.

Robert A. Iger. (n.d.). *The Walt Disney Company*. Retrieved from https://www.thewaltdisneycompany.com/leaders/robert-a-iger/

Rodriguez, A. (2017, January 17). Ten years ago, Netflix launched streaming video and changed the way we watch everything. *Quartz*. Retrieved from https://qz.com/887010/netflix-nflx-launched-streaming-video-10-years-ago-and-changed-the-way-we-watch-everything/

Rothman, W. (2004, February 26). 'DVD's? I Don't Rent. I Own', *The New York Times*, E1–E6.

Sherman, A. (2020, December 8). AT&T has added 4 Million HBO Max subscribers since September 30, CEO John Stankey says. *CNBC*. Retrieved from https://www.cnbc.com/2020/12/08/att-has-added-4-million-hbo-max-subscribers-since-sept-30.html

Silva, R. (2020, February 6). All about the Netflix streaming service. *Lifewire*. Retrieved from https://www.lifewire.com/overview-of-the-netflix-streaming-service-1847831

Spangler, T. (2017, February 21). MLB, Disney tap Amazon's Michael Paull as CEO of BAMTech Streaming Venture. *Variety*. Retrieved from https://variety.com/2017/digital/news/michael-paull-ceo-bamtech-mlbam-disney-1201992713/

Spangler, T. (2021, June 1). Warner Bros. Discovery's initial logo for Wordmark mocked online. *Variety*. Retrieved from https://variety.com/2021/digital/news/warner-bros-discovery-logo-mocked-1234985685/

Spangler, T. (2022, August 4). Paramount+ tops 43 million subscribers in Q2, adding 3.7 million in quarter. *Variety*. Retrieved from https://variety.com/2022/digital/news/paramount-plus-q2-2022-subscribers-1235332550/

Statz, P. (2006, September 8). Amazon Unbox gets it all wrong. *Wired*. Retrieved from https://www.wired.com/2006/09/amazon-unbox-gets-it-all-wrong/

Stewart, J. (2006). *Disney war*. New York: Simon and Schuster.

Storey, K. (2017, February 14). Disney looks to take full ownership of its failing Paris resort. *Orlando Weekly*. Retrieved from https://www.orlandoweekly.com/Blogs/archives/2017/02/14/disney-looks-to-take-full-ownership-of-its-failing-paris-resort

Strange, A. (2021, November 24). As streamers pare down their subscriptions, Disney+ may be the most at risk. Quartz. Retrieved from https://qz.com/2094039/why-disney-subscriber-growth-has-slowed-post-pandemic/

Susanin, T., & Miller, D. (2011). *Walt before Mickey: Disney's early years, 1919–1928*. Jackson, MS: The University Press of Mississippi.

Thomas, B. (1994). *An American original: Walt Disney*. Glendale, CA: Disney Editions.

Trenholm, R. (2019, October 31). Apple TV Plus reviews: Are the new shows any good? *CNET*. Retrieved from https://www.cnet.com/news/apple-tv-plus-shows-reviews-the-morning-show-see-for-all-mankind/

Turow, J. (1997). *Media systems in society: Understanding industries, strategies, and power*. New York: Longman.

Van Maanen, J. (1992). Displacing Disney: Some notes on the flow of culture. *Qualitative Sociology*, *15*(1), 5–35.

Wasko, J. (2001). *Understanding Disney* (1st ed.). Malden, MA: Polity.

Wasko, J. (2020). *Understanding Disney* (2nd ed.). Malden, MA: Polity.

Webb, K. (2020, September 22). NBC's new streaming service, Peacock, is now available on Roku devices—here's how to sign up. *Business Insider*. Retrieved from https://www.businessinsider.com/peacock-streaming-service

Wolf, M. (1999). *The entertainment economy: How mega-media forces are transforming our lives*. New York: Random House.

2 Him Too

John Lasseter's Sexism and the Simple Solution of *Purl*

When Tamara Burke first coined the phrase "Me Too," she was posting to the old social media platform MySpace, and her reference was to the problem of workplace sexual harassment and assault generally. She was not singling out a specific industry. Yet, when *The New York Times* broke their story about Harvey Weinstein's sordid history of sexual harassment and abuse on October 5, 2017, it inspired the phrase to be adopted as a Twitter hashtag (#MeToo), as more women working in the media industry came forward with their stories, some of which involved Weinstein directly. What came to light about Weinstein was a history of gross misconduct that some regarded as an open secret in the media industry (Kantor & Twohey, 2017). The story reflected the very core of the #MeToo movement. It documents how a man would use his power to provide himself opportunities for sexual assault and then use that same power to silence the victims. When that did not work, he would just have his company pay the women to drop their allegations. After the story broke and more accusers came forward, Weinstein ultimately had to face criminal charges and was convicted of rape and sexual assault.

Disney executives were undoubtedly glad they were no longer associated with the notorious media figure. Although Disney had bought out Weinstein's company Miramax in 1993, Harvey and his brother Bob had left Miramax to form the Weinstein Company in 2005. In other words, Harvey was no longer their problem. A month later, however, Disney would indeed have their own problem when a November 21, 2017 story in *The New York Times* disclosed that John Lasseter, the Chief Creative Officer for Walt Disney Animation and Pixar, would be taking a six-month "leave of absence" due to charges of sexual misconduct (Barnes, 2017).

According to the story, those charges came to light when Rashida Jones, an actress who was working as a writer on *Toy Story 4* (2019), stepped away from the project due to what was rumored to be unwanted sexual advances by Lasseter. In a statement to *The New York Times*, Jones and her writing partner, Will McCormick, would deny their departure was due to any "unwanted advances." However, they aver that Pixar had a "culture where women and people of color do not have an equal voice" (Barnes, 2017, para. 9). The story points out that with 19 films under its

DOI: 10.4324/9781003364658-2

belt, Pixar has only employed one female director, and she was fired before her project, *Brave* (2012), was completed.

In her story for *The Hollywood Reporter* (published on the same day), Kim Masters goes into greater detail about Lasseter's behavior. Unnamed sources at Pixar related several incidents where Lasseter would touch female employees who worked at the studio in inappropriate ways. One source mentioned that a photo displayed in the company offices depicting Lasseter standing between two women, was carefully cropped so that it did not reveal where he was touching the women. Lasseter's inappropriate behavior had become such a standard part of the corporate culture that women began calling a move designed to block Lasseter from touching their legs "The Lasseter" (Masters, 2017). One of the important aspects of organizational culture is the use of special terminology or jargon that has a specific meaning within the organization (Martin, 2002). In this case, "The Lasseter" was a term that, while perhaps meaningless outside of Pixar, had meaning within the studio, a meaning that both signified the culture Lasseter created and a practice the female employees developed in order to survive in that culture.

Bob Iger relates how he dealt with the complaints about Lasseter in a relatively brief passage in his book; a total of three paragraphs are devoted to the incident. Iger admits that he had spoken to Lasseter before about his behavior, but in "the fall of 2017. . . it was clear to me that he had to be confronted" (2019, p. 204). Iger and Alan Horn (Chief Creative Officer at Disney) agreed that Lasseter should take a leave of absence, and in his absence, "we put a leadership structure in place at Pixar and Disney Animation and we conducted dozens of interviews with people at both studios to determine what was best for the organization" (2019, p. 205). But if Lasseter's departure created a problem in the leadership structure, the problems he created within the organizational culture may not have been as easily rectified.

In a guest column for *Variety*, Cassandra Smolcic, a former graphic designer, revealed that Lasseter's actions enabled a sexist culture that permeated Pixar Studios. When she started at Pixar as an intern, Smolcic felt that she had landed her dream job. However, she soon discovered that she was mistaken when she received warnings about Lasseter's inappropriate behavior with female employees. Two weeks into her internship, she had an encounter with a department head who, like Lasseter, had a reputation for sexually harassing women in the company. Although Smolcic had been warned about him too, she still found his sexual advances disturbing. She goes on to describe a work environment that resembled a college fraternity, populated by "'manolescent' peers in Hawaiian shirts and graphic tees" (2018, para. 9). As Smolcic maintains:

> At Pixar, my female-ness was an undeniable impediment to my value, professional mobility, and sense of security within the company. The stress of working amidst such a blatantly sexist atmosphere took its toll and was a major factor in forcing me out of the industry.
>
> (2018, para. 3)

She holds Lasseter responsible for setting a low bar for the treatment of women at Pixar studios and for serving as the prime agent in creating a sexist culture.

Given this culture, it is interesting to note that one of the first Pixar shorts to appear on Disney+, entitled *Purl,* relates the experiences of a female ball of pink yarn at a company called B.R.O Capital. Contextualized in relation to the reports about Lasseter and Pixar's corporate culture, it is easy to see parallels with the environment depicted in this short. Indeed, the film's creator, Kristen Lester, was very specific about her purpose:

> A few times during my career in animation, I would be in situations similar to those in the short and I would feel very alone. . . I hoped that by making the short, people would watch and know that they are not alone and that being accepted for who you are is possible.
>
> (Leach, 2019, para. 5)

Given the responses on Twitter, it would seem that Lester's purpose was realized. Amanda Clack (2019) tweeted: "This Disney Pixar film nails what it's like to be the only woman in the office but shows how pioneers can make a cultural impact for the better." Kendra Lee (2019) offers the following praise: "With #Purl, Pixar shows us how workplace cultures are built – exclusion and norming are contagious. The good news: so is inclusion. We each can decide what behaviors we want to support." There were some women who even posted to Twitter pictures of themselves in *Purl* cosplay, embodying their identification with the character.

While critics noted that *Purl* was a bit unorthodox for Pixar, given that many of the characters curse and tell sexist jokes, they also praised the film for its feminist take on workplace culture. Emily Canal (2019), a staff writer for *Inc.*, argues that the film reveals truths about the lack of workplace diversity and the failure of companies to prevent toxic work cultures and employee alienation. On *Mashable*, Proma Khosla remarks that *Purl* is a "powerful story about the difficulty of fitting into a workplace of human males . . . a transparent allegory for women trying to break the glass ceiling in corporate culture" (2019, para. 1). Molly Freeman, writing for *Screen Rant*, also hailed *Purl* as a "feminist allegory" and relates it to the controversy surrounding John Lasseter:

> Though *Purl* does not tackle behavior like Lasseter's head-on, the short film addresses certain folks, particularly women, feeling ostracized in male-centric workplaces. Both are, arguably, different symptoms for the same overarching problem in Hollywood and other male-dominated industries.
>
> (2019, para. 6)

We agree with Freeman that Lasseter's behavior and the ostracization of women in the workplace are both symptoms of male-dominated cultures, but we are less certain about *Purl* as a feminist text. While we find the film is well-crafted and provides a humorous and entertaining take on workplace culture problems, it does little to examine those problems. We would argue that the problem with *Purl* is that it is a classic Disney film and thus provides a simple, happy ending to a very complex and ongoing problem. In fact, we will maintain in this chapter that *Purl* does a better job of recuperating the Pixar and Disney brands than it does addressing the problems of toxic masculinity in the workplace.

Pixar's practice of creating content that both entertains and propagates a brand message has been well documented. Robert Alan Brookey and Robert Westerfelhaus (2005) argued in their analysis of the *Monster's Inc.* (2001) DVD that Pixar used the extra features to distinguish itself as a media brand. As they observe, in these features, Pixar simultaneously positions itself as a separate brand, one that supplants Disney's position in the animation market. They also note that Steve Jobs explicitly identified this purpose in his efforts to promote Pixar. In an analysis of *Wall-E* (2008), Maria Bose (2017) has shown how the film imbues the Pixar brand with cultural and environmentally responsible qualities. She also relates these branding efforts to those used to position Apple as a company focused on sustainable practices. By tracing a narrative line through the *Toy Story* trilogy, Jerome Christensen argues these three films articulate Pixar's distinct culture while also illustrating how that culture can be reconciled with the older and more established Disney corporate culture. He notes, however, that Lasseter figures prominently in efforts to integrate these cultures:

> Indeed, rather than facilitating the imposition of Disney ideology on Pixar, the merger has been followed by influence heading the other way – and significantly, not only on the animators. Lasseter is now the principal creative adviser for the Imagineers, who is responsible for planning the future of Disney in all areas of its enterprise.
>
> (2012, Pixar's Logic, para. 26)

Christensen was writing about Pixar well before the news about Lasseter broke, but he illustrates a point that we would like to stress. Although Disney may have dodged a bullet with Weinstein, the Lasseter scandal hit them squarely between the eyes. Lasseter had become the brand ambassador for Disney and Pixar, and he signified the relationship between the two companies. In other words, Lasseter had become a big problem for both Pixar and Disney, one that *Purl* attempts to solve.

This chapter is divided into three parts. In the next section, we provide a brief history of the relationship between Pixar and Disney to show how deeply Lasseter figures into that history. We then offer a textual analysis of *Purl* that identifies how the story conveys a narrative about women's difficulties in the male-dominated work environment. We show how the film reflects several elements of the Classic Disney style and how the adherence to some of these elements limit the film's efforts to convey the problems of toxic masculinity in organizational culture (or to offer a realistic solution to those problems). We then conclude by discussing how Lasseter's actions may have been enabled by cultures already in place at both Disney and Pixar. While *Purl* is our primary object of analysis, we will be considering other Pixar and Disney texts to establish context, as those texts give us insight into the working conditions at both companies.

Pixar, Disney, and Lasseter

Although we now regard Pixar as one of the most visible brands of computer-generated image animation (CGI), its history is a bit more complex. To begin with, the basis for what would become the company started out as a graduate project completed by Ed Catmull, a PhD student in computer science at the University of Utah. In 1972, Catmull completed a computer-animated model of his hand using a 3-D computer program that he authored himself. The animation is available on YouTube, and although it is rendered in black and white and looks very primitive, at the time it was a remarkable feat. When he graduated with his doctorate, computer animation and computer graphics jobs were rare, and he failed to land an academic position. Instead, Catmull worked as a programmer until he was hired by the New York Institute of Technology in 1974 to direct the school's Computer Graphics Lab. Two California artists with an interest in computer graphics soon joined Catmull (Alvy Smith and David DiFrancesco), and along with Catmull's former co-worker Malcolm Blanchard, the four would form what would later become Pixar (Price, 2008).

In 1979 the lab was contacted by a representative of George Lucas. Lucas was increasingly interested in computers as special effects tools. Although *Star Wars* (1977) appeared to have incorporated CGI, in fact, all of the imagery was created using analog equipment, so Lucas was interested in creating a computer graphics lab as part of Lucasfilm. After meeting with Lucas, Catmull accepted a position heading the Lucasfilm Computer Division, and after some rather devious maneuvering, Catmull hired away members of his New York Institute of Technology staff to join him. Ironically, the first significant CGI project produced by the division did not appear in a *Star Wars* film and instead was incorporated into *Star Trek II: The Wrath of Kahn* (1982). In fact, except for some brief scenes in *Return of the Jedi* (1983), the division was not asked to contribute much to actual film production. Catmull, however, was approached by John Lasseter, who was employed at Disney at the time. Lasseter was working on an animated adaptation of the children's book *The Brave Little Toaster* (1987), and he was interested in combining computer animation with traditional animation for the project. Disney, however, paused the project and laid off Lasseter. Catmull, encouraged by Smith, hired Lasseter to join his division at Lucasfilm (Price, 2008).

Around this time, unfortunately, George Lucas had seemed to lose interest in the Computer Division, and his marriage was also coming to an end. Lucas had met his wife Marcia, a film editor, in the late 1960s, and they had been married for 14 years. Marcia was a very accomplished film editor in her own right, working on *Alice Doesn't Live Here Anymore* (1974), *Taxi Driver* (1976), and George's own *American Graffiti* (1973). Because of California divorce laws and the fact they had married without a prenuptial agreement, George and Marcia were required to split their property 50/50. George wanted to maintain ownership and control of Lucasfilm, and Marcia wanted her share in cash, estimated to be $25 million. Consequently, George had to raise cash, and he was looking at selling off some of his assets, including the Computer Division. Steve Jobs, who had just been maneuvered out of his own company, Apple Inc., had a lot of time and cash on his hands. When he visited Lucasfilm, he was impressed by what he saw at the Computer Division but thought George's asking price ($30 million) was too high. Lucas, however, was unable to find another buyer for the division and finally sold it to Jobs for $10 million in February 1986; at this time, Pixar was officially incorporated (Deutschman, 2001).

Initially, Jobs was not that involved in the operation at Pixar, and he rarely visited the company's offices (Deutschman, 2001). When Jobs acquired the company, it was trying to position itself in the market as a hardware manufacturer with the Pixar Image Computer, which sold for $135,000. Given that high price point, the market for this product was very limited. In fact, Disney was their best client, and the company used Pixar's Computer Animation Production System (CAPS) to add texture and detail to scenes that appeared in *The Little Mermaid* (1989) and *The Rescuers Down Under* (1990). Still, Catmull and Smith were having difficulty demonstrating the value of the Pixar computer, and that is when Lasseter demonstrated his value. Lasseter was tasked with developing short animated films produced on the Pixar Image Computer, and these films began gaining attention. Lasseter was responsible for developing and producing *Luxo Jr.* (1986), an animated short that would introduce the character that would become integral to Pixar's brand identity: the lamp is featured in the Pixar logo, their answer to Disney's Mickey Mouse. The short secured for Lasseter a reputation of understanding the capabilities of computer animation and understanding and executing the principles of good storytelling, principles he learned from Disney (Price, 2008).

As we mentioned earlier, before coming to Pixar, Lasseter worked in animation at Disney, but his history with the company goes even further back. Although he was always fascinated by cartoons, his interest in pursuing a career in animation was piqued when he came across Disney animator Bob Thomas' 1958 book *The Art of Animation.* He applied to CalArts (the school established by Walt and Roy Disney), was accepted, and began studying animation at the school in 1975. He would work at Disneyland during his summers, where he was a ride operator on the Jungle Cruise ride.

Disney hired him after graduating from CalArts, where he worked until he was let go and hired by Pixar (Price, 2008).

While studying at CalArts and working at Disney, Lasseter learned how Walt Disney found the comic value in imbuing inanimate objects with human emotion. Lasseter took that principle a step further to create animated inanimate objects that could also render dramatic emotions (Price, 2008). This realization would inspire his creation of *Luxo Jr.*, and Lasseter would also apply the extended principle to the production of *Tin Toy* (1988), an animated short that would secure Pixar's first Oscar. This success piqued Disney's interest in producing a computer-animated feature film.

Disney already had a working relationship with Pixar (thanks to their use of CAPS and the Pixar Image Computer), so they decided to approach the company about a partnership. Lasseter's visibility and the fact that he was a CalArts graduate with experience working with Disney were most likely also an advantage for Pixar. Indeed, when Jeffery Katzenberg, who at the time was in charge of Disney film production (including animation), began negotiating with Pixar, he made it clear that he felt Lasseter was the creative driving force behind the animation upstart (Price, 2008). After a series of negotiations, the two companies signed a contract in July 1991. The contract was a three-picture deal that was decidedly in Disney's favor: Disney would own all film rights (including rights to any sequels or spin-offs) and would receive significantly more revenue from the productions than Pixar. The first film to be produced under the contract was, of course, *Toy Story*, and Lasseter would serve as the director for the film. *Toy Story* met and exceeded expectations and was the third highest-grossing film of 1995, following *Batman Forever* (1995) and *Apollo 13* (1995).[1]

Emboldened by this success, Steve Jobs renegotiated Pixar's contract with Disney to share production and marketing costs. While both companies would also receive equal billing in all advertising and product tie-ins, Disney would retain a distribution fee as a percentage of box office receipts. Even under the new contract, Disney would make more money off of Pixar's films than Pixar. The first picture under the new contract would be *A Bug's Life* which grossed $363 million worldwide. This was followed *by Toy Story 2* (1999) and *Monsters Inc.*, which generated $487 million and $632 million in worldwide box office receipts, respectively.

As Pixar's visibility increased, so did Lasseter's. Jobs promoted him to a position as vice president for creative development about the time Pixar had its IPO. As Jobs maneuvered to position the company as a recognizable media brand, Lasseter functioned as the brand ambassador. As we mentioned earlier, Brookey and Westerfelhaus (2006) identified the efforts to assert the Pixar brand in their analysis of the *Monsters Inc.* DVD special features. Although they argue that the company distinguishes itself by its collaborative creative efforts, it is important to note how Lasseter serves as the primary source of the brand message. For example, in a feature entitled *Pixar Fun Factory* (2002), the video begins with Lasseter identifying himself as the director of all the previous Pixar films, and he welcomes the audience on a tour of Pixar's new facilities. On this tour, we meet Pete Docter (the director of *Monsters Inc.*), Andrew Gordon, Joe Ranft, Lee Unrich, David Silverman (co-director of *Monsters Inc.*), John Kahrs, and Glenn McQueen; we are introduced to only one woman, Darla Anderson, the producer of *Monsters Inc.*

Although other women appear in the frame of this feature, none of them are introduced, and it is worth noting how well *Pixar Fun Factory* illustrates the culture alluded to by Smolcic. Most of the Pixar staff are wearing Hawaiian shirts, and throughout the feature, the men are often engaged in what could be described as "manolescent" behavior. They are often riding around on razor scooters (which were popular at the time); they are shown playing foosball, miniature golf, and participating in a paper airplane competition. Although women might have participated in this competition, none are shown. And as if to announce his own agency in creating this culture, we are taken into Lasseter's office, where the shelves are filled with toys (many of which appear to be Pixar ancillary products). He looks straight into the camera and says, "I love toys!" As for a climate in which women were devalued, there is an editing choice in the feature that is remarkable. At one point, Lasseter observes in a voice-over, "Our people work so hard. They work really long hours making these movies. But number one to us, is to make a great movie that audiences around the world will enjoy." During this voice-over, we are shown several men working, and we are not shown any women (with the possible exception of women sitting passively, while watching a man pitch a story idea).

At the time of the making of this feature, Pixar had yet to be acquired by Disney. In fact, Pixar had not yet released what would prove to be (at the time) its most substantial hit: *Finding Nemo,* which would set new box office records for an animated feature with a $962 million worldwide take. Once again emboldened by the success of Pixar's films, Jobs set out to renegotiate the contract with Disney, but this time he was not as successful. Primarily the problem was Michael Eisner, who did not want to provide Pixar with more favorable terms. He insisted that *Toy Story 2* was still under the original contract terms, arguing that it was a sequel. In addition to Eisner's recalcitrance, Jobs was displeased with what he regarded as Eisner's disrespect for Pixar's creative contributions. Jobs broke off negotiations and began shopping the other studios for a more favorable deal. The news came as another blow to Eisner, at a time when he was already confronting efforts to oust him from the company (Stewart, 2006). As we noted in the first chapter, those efforts would ultimately prove successful, and Eisner was replaced by Bob Iger. One of Iger's first moves was to acquire Pixar outright.

This acquisition, though significant for a variety of reasons, would prove most significant for Lasseter. Once the deal was finalized, Jobs would join the Disney board, and Lasseter would be appointed Chief Creative Officer of both Pixar and Walt Disney Animation Studios. In important ways, this was a homecoming for Lasseter, given that his first jobs were at Disney, and his own education in animation was heavily influenced and arguably provided by the company. In fact, Lasseter would become the nexus point that would tie Pixar to Disney both culturally and organizationally. Because of Lasseter, Pixar was, in several respects, always already a Disney Company, even before it had been acquired.

Although Ed Catmull would also obtain an important position after the acquisition and become President of Pixar and Disney Animation, he executed his duties behind the scenes and allowed Lasseter to assume a much more public role. In fact, in his book chronicling the history of Pixar, David Price (2008) begins with Lasseter's first presentation to the Disney shareholders following the acquisition. As he recounts Lasseter's presentation, Lasseter then introduces Catmull to the shareholders, and it is then that Price first mentions Catmull. This opening passage speaks to the fact that while both men enjoyed influential roles governing both Pixar and Disney Animation, Lasseter was much more visible as a spokesperson. Given Lasseter's visibility and importance to both companies and their relationship, Disney had a big problem on its hands when the reports of sexual harassment and sexism emerged. And this is when *Purl* enters the scene.

Purl One, Sexism Zero

When Disney+ launched, it included among its Pixar offerings a series of short animated films called SparkShorts. These are films produced by Pixar animators, and those animators, while given a limited budget and a shorter production schedule, are also given complete freedom to develop their stories and execute the films. As Dirk Libbey observed in *Cinemablend*, "As a result of this creative freedom, SparksShorts tend to be incredibly personal works, much more so than anything we've seen from Pixar's theatrical output" (2019, para. 10). Consequently, the stories represented in these short films also reflect a diverse set of experiences. For example, *Float* (2019), from writer/producer Bobby Rubio, chronicles a Filipino father's attempt to hide his son who has a tendency to float into the air. It provides a brief, yet emotional, representation of a father's struggle to accept his child's difference. *Wind* (2019), directed by Edwin Chang, captures the experience of a grandmother and grandson who struggle to escape from a dark chasm. While the boy escapes, the grandmother is left behind; a poignant reminder that class mobility is not always realized equally among family members. *Out* (2020), written and directed by Steven Clay Hunter, introduced Pixar's first lead gay character, and turned the emotional experience of a man coming out to his parents into a slapstick comedy. In a promotional video for the SparkShorts series posted on Facebook, Lindsay Collins, Pixar's Vice President of Development and New Media, describes the purpose of the series this way: "So that's why we call them SparkShorts, and not just Pixar. We wanted to discover that new creative spark, and it allows us to start thinking about the future storytellers, the future directors, the future producers" (SparkShorts, 2019).

As we noted earlier, *Purl* was directed by Kristen Lester and related her own experiences as a woman working in animation. Her story may have been informed by her experiences working at Pixar under Lasseter (her LinkedIn profile indicates that she joined the studio in 2012), but Lester has worked at other animation studios as well, including Bluesky Illumination and the Cartoon Network. In any event, Lester's *Purl*, like the other SparkShorts, is a personal story.

Purl opens with a shot of the offices of B.R.O. Capital, a space fully occupied by men, all wearing dark suits and white shirts, chatting by the printer, arguing in a conference room, and exchanging such greetings as "See you at the gym tonight." We then have a shot of "Drew" entering an elevator, providing orientation to what we assume is a new employee. Drew, however, is focused on his phone and interrupts the orientation to mention that "The Tigers are up by 20, yes!" He finally glances at the name tag of this new employee, and it is then he realizes that B.R.O. Capital has hired a pink ball of yarn named Purl. Purl expresses her excitement about joining the company and that she still thinks, "it's unbelievable that I'm even here." Drew, upon reflection, agrees and quickly sends a text on his phone.

Purl's optimism is soon tempered when the elevator opens on a floor populated by men in dark suits, who regard her with shock and disbelief. As one of them remarks while he checks his phone, possibly receiving Drew's text, "Did you see they hired a ball of . . . yo?" He is struck speechless once he sees Purl. As she sets up her desk, with a green knitting bag, a pink and yellow knitted plant, a purple knitted desk cover, and a bright blue pen cup, Purl introduces a variety of color into an office interior that is made up of dark and neutral colors. The male co-workers look at her with confusion and suspicion, while three of them tell jokes around the water cooler, "What's the difference between a porcupine and a BMW? With the porcupine, the pricks are on the outside." Purl attempts to join the conversation by telling a knitting joke, and it is not well received. "Is that like a sport or something?" one of them asks.

Later at a staff meeting, one of them remarks, "As you can see, we have a big failure on our hands." The camera focuses on a presentation slide with the word "Failure" in bright red letters; above the word is a bright pink pie chart graphic that resembles Purl in both shape and color. During the meeting, Purl suggests a strategy could be found through a collaboration with finance. This suggestion is dismissed out of hand, as "Too soft, we gotta be aggressive." Purl then is literally spun out of the meeting as the male employees at B.R.O Capital decide to go for "Wings at Swifties."

As they all load onto the elevator, someone asks, "Is that everybody?" Drew replies as he looks back at Purl dismissively, "That's everybody." He then closes the elevator door, and Purl is left behind, alone in the office. She begins packing up her desk, removes her nametag, and then looks at a wall where the B.R.O Capital Team photos are displayed. They all face the same direction in their photos, they all have the same tight smile, and they all are wearing the customary dark suits with white shirts. Purl gets an idea and goes into the restroom to knit herself into a gray suit; she has also flattened her shape so that she looks more like the men in the office.

Her efforts pay off. Later at the water cooler, she tells another joke that lands nicely with her co-workers: "So then he says, I know this suit is expensive, baby, but at my apartment, it's 100% off!" Then at another staff meeting, the presentation slide show includes another graphic that resembles the new Purl, with the word "Success" along the bottom of the graphic. Purl now is the one to first argue for an aggressive strategy in the meeting, "I say we go for it, and if finance doesn't like it, they can kiss our ass!" Her new approach is well received, and this time Purl is invited to happy hour at Swifties.

What follows is a video montage of Purl imagining herself in a night out on the town with her co-workers, attending a sporting event, drinking too much, and then vomiting green yarn. All the while, her co-workers cheer her on. Then the elevator doors open to relieve a new employee, a ball of yellow yarn, who seems to blather on about her difficulties finding the office. Purl says derisively to her co-workers, "Leave the knitting at your nana's house." And just as they are about ready to leave this new employee behind to head to Swifties, Purl experiences a pang of empathy as she looks at her employee ID with the picture of her former self. She is reminded that she was once a ball of yarn and steps off the elevator to invite the new employee, "Lacy," to join them. She introduces Lacy to the men on the elevator who regard her with suspicion.

The next scene opens in the same elevator, but this time a man is the new employee, and Purl is the one who welcomes him to B.R.O. Capital. When the doors open on the office, it is now filled with brightly colored balls of yarn, making up a visual rainbow of diversity. The men are there too, but now some are just in shirt sleeves, and some are wearing colored shirts. One of them asks Purl if she is going to "Swifties tonight?" Her reply: "Is a wool sweater scratchy?" This time her yarn joke lands, and the credits begin to roll.

In important ways, *Purl* reflects several elements of the Classic Disney style as identified by Wasko (2001), specifically light entertainment, anthropomorphized characters, innocence, individualism, stereotypical gender representation, and optimism. The short is clearly in the realm of light entertainment, and although some of the jokes are highly sexualized, those jokes function as markers for the environment that Purl must navigate. While her navigation may lead her to adopt some of those sexist mores, those mores seem to be abandoned in the resolution of the narrative that leads to a happy ending. In addition to the gendering of her color (pink), Purl, as a character, is an anthropomorphized marker for an activity that is coded as feminine, hence the numerous knitting puns. When she denigrates that activity in reference to Lacy, it is at that moment she realizes she is denigrating her own character, a realization she has when she contemplates her true form captured in the picture on her name tag. That same anthropomorphism is then used to represent the successful diversification of the B.R.O. Capital workplace, as the office is now populated by several brightly colored balls of yarn.

Purl enters into B.R.O. Capital, and the narrative, with a sense of innocence. Although this innocence is soon lost when she adopts her corporate persona, she is reminded of that lost innocence when Lacy appears on the scene. It becomes her point of empathy with Lacy. Interestingly, when Purl tries to adapt to the corporate culture, she loses her individualism, but that loss functions as the stakes in the conflict. In other words, her reassertion of her individualism also signifies her triumph over her conflict with the B.R.O. Capital culture, and that same reassertion secures a more diverse environment for the company. Yet, the characteristics of Purl's individualism also seem to reflect stereotypical gender norms that are also associated with the Classic Disney style. Purl's disruptive presence may be due to her gender, but that gender is coded by a bright shade of pink, while the males in the office are gendered by the dark colors of their suits. Therefore, if, as critics have asserted, Purl is a feminist figure, then she is one that is bright pink and continually references the practice of knitting. Those facts do not necessarily prevent Purl from serving as the protagonist in a feminist allegory, but her representation as a gendered figure is, at the very least, stereotypical and therefore problematic.

More problematic, however, is how the short reflects the optimism associated with the Classic Disney style; her optimism distinguishes the character of Purl, and that same optimism seems to inform the resolution of the conflict in the scene. The reformation of B.R.O Capital comes from a simple decision to invite the new yellow ball of yarn, Lacy, to join Purl and the guys at Swifties. This decision plays out in a brief moment of recognition in which Purl empathizes with the new employee and then realizes that she can draw on her recent acceptance in the company to expand acceptance generally. The final scene seems to play that out, with Purl now back to her original pink form, showing a new employee the new, clearly more diverse company. This resolution is not only optimistic, but it is also exceedingly simplistic. Unfortunately, sexist corporate culture is not so easily overcome.

As Jesper B. Sørensen has observed, "Firms with strong cultures incur a tradeoff with respect to their adaptive ability in the face of environmental change. Strong corporate cultures facilitate reliable performances in relatively stable environments, but as volatility increases, these benefits are dramatically attenuated" (2002, p. 88). In other words, changes can prove disruptive for established corporate cultures, and therefore strong corporate cultures are often resistant to change. Indeed, corporate culture can be a strong, enabling force for sexual harassment to occur and continue, especially in male-dominated corporate environments (MacDonald, 2012).

To this degree, Lester correctly characterized this type of corporate culture in her rendering of B.R.O. capital. What she gets wrong is the ease with which these kinds of corporate cultures can be changed.

Granted, *Purl* is merely an eight-minute animated film, and therefore offers a narrative arc that is too limited in scope to convey the complexities of sexism in corporate culture.

Yet, as we noted earlier, many people praised *Purl* for addressing the difficulties women encounter in the workplace. We do not want to diminish the experiences of women who relate to the film, particularly to the degree that the film reflects those difficulties. However, we feel that it is important to observe how quickly and simply those difficulties are overcome in *Purl,* and note how this simplicity is where the film stumbles as a feminist allegory. In other words, the fact that *Purl* is too limited in scope is precisely our point.

The audience is never shown what takes place after Purl invites Lacy along to Swifties. Instead, we are left to assume that the comradery over wings and drinks at the bar leads to a significant cultural shift at the company. That is a lot to assume, given the literature that indicates a cultural change in companies is sometimes not easy to achieve. These problems can be compounded when the senior management stands in opposition to the victims of sexual harassment or attempts to bribe and intimidate those victims who come forward with complaints (MacDonald, 2012), which brings us back to the case of Harvey Weinstein. By many accounts, the other employees who worked at Miramax, and later the Weinstein company, felt powerless to stop Weinstein's behavior and felt guilty over their inaction when victims were being intimidated. In the documentary *Untouchable* (2019), several of Weinstein's former employees are interviewed and report on the difficulties they experienced in confronting him about his treatment of women. Some acknowledge their complicity by remaining silent. Others recount how they were also personally and legally intimidated by Weinstein when they tried to challenge him or support his victims.

In Lasseter's case, while his actions were not felonious, he too enjoyed great power in establishing the culture at Pixar. While the employees at Pixar were aware of the problem, including Iger, it was dealt with through accommodation; for example, rather than punishing Lasseter for inappropriately touching women, employees would simply crop out the photographic evidence. In fact, Lasseter's example shows why the narrative resolution offered in *Purl* should be regarded with suspicion. Social events involving alcohol, just like the evenings at Swifties if we are to believe Purl's imagination, were precisely the situation in which Lasseter would make a move, literarily; the move that inspired the female employees at Pixar to coin the term "The Lasseter."

Therefore, the optimistic narrative resolution offered in *Purl* not only misrepresents the difficulty in confronting and changing sexist work environments, the solution it does seem to offer (that everything can be worked out over drinks) is the same circumstance in which the female employees at Pixar were most at risk (Masters, 2017). In addition, while the film offers up Purl as the hero of culture change at B.R.O. Capital, this is just another story in which the burden of correcting a sexist culture is assumed not by the perpetrators but by the victims. In this respect, *Purl* again adheres to gender stereotypes in that it falls to women to clean up a mess created by men. Further, the film optimistically represents those efforts as an easy and straightforward solution. In other words, *Purl* fails as a feminist allegory because, in the final analysis, it is just another Classic Disney film.

Yet as a form of brand recuperation, *Purl* seems to have been rather successful. The film was the first of the SparkShorts to be released to the public on February 4, 2019, approximately seven months after Lasseter's departure from Pixar and nine months before the launch of Disney+. Given the time of its release, *Purl* was able to address an embarrassing episode in both Pixar and Disney's recent history while also promoting the streaming service that would be very important to the future of both companies. Admittedly, the animated short is not about Lasseter's actual misbehavior at Pixar, and it is difficult to imagine that Pixar would produce such a film. Instead of producing a film about Pixar, the company did the next best thing; it produced a film *by* Pixar: one that addresses the very issues of sexist workplace culture and gender exclusion for which Lasseter was dismissed. *Purl*, in effect, positions Pixar as a company that now understands the problems of its corporate culture and is ready to correct that culture, and create an environment that is both supportive of women and values diversity. The SparkShorts go a long way in representing Pixar in this way. In fact, in an interview with Delaware Public Media, Collins indicated that gender equity was a primary consideration when the directors were chosen (Schellong, 2019). Therefore, the fact that the first of the SparkShorts films released was created by a female employee (Lester) seems purposeful.

Given that Lester is also identified as a new talent at Pixar and one that Collins would characterize as the future of the company, *Purl* indicates that Lasseter is in the past, and the future of Pixar is both bright and diverse. Given the positive response to *Purl,* it would seem the film has been successful in this regard. Finally, the placement of the film as original content featured on Disney+ suggested to subscribers what they could come to expect from the service. Again, a bright future indeed!

Lasseter, a Company Man to the End

While we believe that *Purl* provided a valuable service to recuperate both Pixar and Disney's brand, it indexed a significant change to both companies in meaningful ways. To the degree that Lasseter served an important role for both Disney and Pixar, his departure was significant to both companies. It heralded a change from the corporate culture for which he had been a prime agent. It would be naïve, however, to think that Lasseter created that culture from whole cloth. In fact, we would maintain that he was enabled by the cultures already in place at both companies.

It is important to remember that Lasseter started as an animator at Disney in 1979 and Pixar in 1983. When he joined Disney, seven of the original "Nine Old Men," a group of animators who had joined the company in its early years, from 1927 to 1935, were still working at the studio. This included Bob Thomas, who had authored the book that inspired Lasseter to pursue a career in animation. In other words, Lasseter joined the company in time to work alongside his role models. The fact that they were proudly referred to as the "Nine Old Men" speaks volumes about how gender figured into the early workplace culture at Disney. Although we would not ascribe any sexual impropriety to this culture, it is clear the company did not imagine that women had an important place in that company.

Indeed, some of the content available on the Disney+ service provides insight into how the studio regarded women. *Waking Sleeping Beauty* (2009), a documentary directed by Disney animator and producer Don Hahn, and the Disney+ original series *The Imagineering Story* (2019), executive produced by Leslie Iwerks (granddaughter of Micky Mouse animator Ub Iwerks), both provide evidence of the male-dominated work culture at the Disney. *Waking Sleeping Beauty* primarily focuses on the Walt Disney Feature Animation division from the years 1984 to 1994. However, the documentary begins prior to this period when Lasseter was still part of the animation staff. Early in the documentary, we are shown an amateurish film of Randy Cartwright (an animator who would go on to work at DreamWorks) providing a tour of the studio and introducing the animation artists; Lasseter holds the camera. Cartwright first introduces the current CEO Ron Miller, and then Ron Clements, John Musker, Glen Keane, Tim Burton, and Joe Ranft. Although we are shown stills of the animation staff, and clearly women were staff members, they are never introduced in the footage we are shown. Instead, Ron Clements, in his narration, characterizes this time as a period of cross-generational transition from the Nine Old Men to the new animators, and over this narration, we are again shown men who illustrate both the old and the new guard.

This representation of a male-dominated culture could be dismissed as a product of editing if it were not for the fact that the issue is dealt with explicitly in *The Imagineering Story*.[2] This series focuses on the evolution of Walt Disney Imagineering from its earlier manifestation as WED Enterprises. It reveals much about the corporate culture and how women were regarded in that culture. For example, Mary Blair, who worked as an animator on *Peter Pan* (1953), *Alice in Wonderland* (1951), and *Cinderella* (1950), was one of the first Imagineers at WED Enterprises. She also served as the lead artist for the iconic It's a Small World ride. As one of her contemporaries, Alice Davis, notes, Mary's contributions were often dismissed unfairly at Disney: "Nobody really appreciated her as much as they should have. People would say, 'oh, she just puts the color down.' "Marty Skyler describes the work environment in the early days of WED as one in which "(t)here were women here, but there were not a lot of them." He also mentions how another of the early female employees, Harriet Burns, adapted to the environment: "I tell you when she was with the boys, she was one of the boys." In other words, it seems Burns adapted to WED Enterprises in a way similar to the way Purl first adjusted to B.R.O. Capital.

The number of women involved in the division would expand as the Imagineers began working on Experimental Prototype Community of Tomorrow (EPCOT) in the mid- to late 1970s. As Peggie Farris, who joined the company as an Imagineer in 1976, observes,

> (t)here weren't many women in executive positions when I arrived... but there were young women who were coming out of architecture school, there were young women who were lighting designers, there were project managers, engineers, and we were all part of this new generation of people.
>
> (Iwerks, 2019)

Although Lasseter was located in animation, he would be part of this new generation, but he joined Disney when it was still a male-dominated work environment.

When Lasseter joined Pixar, the situation was no different. Catmull and Smith were still fully in charge, and this was at a time where Lucas owned the entire operation. In fact, a picture included in Price's book of the computer graphic group of the Lucasfilm Computer Division dated 1984 shows Lasseter standing alongside nine other men; there are no women in the photo, and three other men are listed as "not pictured." Indeed, the situation at Pixar at the time appears to have been worse than it was at Disney because it was a work environment that was exclusively male, with the possible exception of Catmull's secretary, Susan Anderson, whom Catmull would later marry. In other words, during Lasseter's first years at Pixar, women were either secretaries or wives or both.

Therefore, Lasseter was enculturated in workplace environments where men were in charge. He took this enculturation as a cue to create his own male-dominated work environment when he was elevated to a position of power. This is not to excuse his actions but to posit how his actions were enabled. If anything, Lasseter's work history implicates him in his failure to make Pixar (and, in turn, Disney animation) a place that valued women. As for his sexual impropriety, it is essential to note that environments in which women are not valued create the conditions in which they can be treated as sexual objects. Indeed, this is why male-dominated work environments are conducive to sexual harassment, as MacDonald (2012) has observed.

Today Lasseter is part of Pixar and Disney's history, a history they might want to put behind them. What is clear is that Disney has put out messages to acknowledge that while women may not have always been valued at the company, their contributions are valued now; *The Imagineering Story* seems to be part of that messaging. Leslie Iwerks presence as executive producer indicates the message has substance, and her series engages the issues of gender disparity in the workplace in a self-reflexive and critical way that is rather uncharacteristic for a Disney series. Even Iger's biography displays empathy and concern for the victims of workplace sexual harassment. He relates a story of his early years at ABC when a producer exposed his penis to Iger as an act of intimidation. As he writes, "Forty-five years later, I still get angry when I recall that scene. We've become much more aware of the need for fair, equal non-abusive treatment in the workplace, but it has taken too long" (2019, p. 10). *Purl*, then, can be counted among the messages that Disney has produced to indicate that it wants to create a better work environment for all of its employees. Disney+ provides a highly visible platform for that particular message.

Yet, as we have noted, *Purl*, while offering an entertaining take on workplace sexism, one that has resonated with women's experiences, fails to convey the complexities of the problem. Iger is right. Creating environments that welcome and value the contributions of all employees have taken far too long. But given the recalcitrance of organizational culture and the preponderance of sexual impropriety in the media industry specifically, it should not be too surprising that it has taken this long. This is a process that is certainly more involved than a night out with drinks and wings at Swifties, and it takes much longer than eight minutes. Still, Disney seems to have taken Lasseter's improprieties seriously, and the decision to remove him was one that was not informed by the bottom line, given his successful track record. And if this decision reflects a new effort to change the culture at both Pixar and Disney, then *Purl* functions as the face of that new culture.

As for Lasseter, he has landed at Skydance Animation, which produces films for Paramount. In fact, he has been hired as the head of the studio, although he reports to a CEO, David Ellison (Kit, 2019). His new position has not been without controversy. In fact, right after his appointment was announced, Emma Thompson dropped out of providing voice work for a Skydance production. Thompson was quite public about her reasons for leaving the project and outlined them in a letter she published in The *Los Angeles Times*. She concludes the letter by observing:

> I am well aware that centuries of entitlement to women's bodies, whether they like it or not, is not going to change overnight. Or in a year. But I am also aware that if people who have spoken out – like me – do not take this sort of a stand, then things are very unlikely to change at anything like the pace required to protect my daughter's generation.
> (McNamara, 2019)

Given that Lasseter is still with the studio and the project that Thompson quit is stayed in production, arguably, the pace of change may not protect the next generation of women working in the media industries. Iger is right; change has taken too long, and by some indications, it is far from over. For example, Lasseter's Skydance Animation has cut a deal with Apple to release its future films and television productions (Faughnder, 2021). In fact, the very project that Thompson pulled away from, *Luck* (2022), was released on Apple TV+ and select theaters on August 2, 2022. Although Lasseter was a producer, the film was directed by a woman, Peggy Holmes. As to whether this signifies change, we can only hope.

Notes

1 All box office information referenced in this book was taken from Box Office Mojo (https://www.boxofficemojo.com).
2 We would also maintain that editing as a practice reveals ideological choices, and feminist film criticism has demonstrated how those choices index gender relations.

References

Barnes, B. (2017, November 21). John Lasseter, a Pixar founder, Takes Leave After 'Missteps.' *The New York Times.* Retrieved from https://www.nytimes.com/2017/11/21/business/media/john-lasseter-pixar-disney-leave.html?_r=0

Bose, M. (2017). Immaterial thoughts: Brand value, environmental sustainability, and Wall-E. *Criticism, 59*(2), 247–277.

Brookey, R., & Westerfelhaus, R. (2005). The digital auteur: Branding identity on the Monsters, Inc. DVD. *Western Journal of Communication, 69*(2), 109–128.

Canal, E. (2019, February 14). In an 8-minute animated film, Pixar just captured why companies still struggle with workplace diversity. *Inc.* Retrieved from: https://www.inc.com/emily-canal/pixar-short-purl-workplace-diversity-inclusion.html

Christensen, J. (2012). *America's corporate art: The studio authorship of Hollywood motion pictures.* Stanford, CA: Stanford University Press. [Kindle version]. Retrieved from Amazon.com.

Clack, A. [@amanda_clack]. (2019, February 9). *This Disney Pixar film nails what it's like to be the only woman in the office but shows how pioneers* [Tweet]. Twitter. Retrieved from https://twitter.com/amanda_clack/status/1094237544466796545

Deutschman, A. (2001). *The second coming of Steve Jobs.* New York: Broadway Books.

Faughnder, R. (2021, February 17). John Lasseter-run Skydance Animation sets Apple movie and TV deal. *Los Angeles Times.* Retrieved from https://www.latimes.com/entertainment-arts/business/story/2021-02-17/john-lasseter-run-skydance-animation-sets-apple-movie-and-tv-deal#

Freeman, M. (2019, February 4). Pixar's first SparksShorts short film is a feminist allegory- with yarn. *Screen Rant.* Retrieved from https://screenrant.com/pixar-purl-short-film-sparkshorts/

Iger, B. (2019). *The ride of a lifetime: Lessons learned from 15 years as CEO of the Walt Disney Company.* New York: Random House.

Iwerks, L. (Producer & Director). (2019). *The Imagineering story* (Motion Picture). Burbank, CA: Walt Disney Studios Motion Pictures.

Kantor, J., & Twohey, M. (2017, October 50). Harvey Weinstein paid off sexual harassment accusers for decades. *The New York Times*. Retrieved from https://www.nytimes.com/2017/10/05/us/harvey-weinstein-harassment-allegations.html

Khosla, P. (2019, February 4). Pixar's newest short is a must watch for every workplace. *Mashable*. Retrieved from https://mashable.com/video/pixar-purl-short/#yPuEynpkzEqS

Kit, B. (2019). John Lasseter to head animation for Skydance. *The Hollywood Reporter*. Retrieved from https://www.hollywoodreporter.com/heat-vision/john-lasseter-lead-animation-skydance-1174878h

Leach, S. (2019, February 11). Pixar's new short film *Purl* takes on toxic bro culture at work. *Glamour*. Retrieved from https://www.glamour.com/story/pixar-new-short-film-purl

Lee, K. [@agirlwho_reads]. (2019, February 16). *With #Purl, Pixar shows us how workplace cultures are built – exclusion and norming are contagious. The good news: so is inclusion* [Tweet]. Twitter. Retrieved from https://twitter.com/agirlwho_reads/status/1096760734346731523

Libbey, D. (2019, November 7). Why Pixar's SparkShorts series might not be what Disney fans expect. *Cinemablend*. Retrieved from https://www.cinemablend.com/television/2484070/Why-Pixars-SparkShorts-Series-Might-Not-Be-What-Disney-Fans-Expect

MacDonald, P. (2012). Workplace sexual harassment 30 years on: A review of the literature. *International Journal of Management Review, 14*, 1–17.

Martin, J. (2002). *Organizational Culture: Mapping the Terrain*. Thousand Oaks, CA: Sage Publications.

Masters, K. (2017, November 21). John Lasseter's pattern of misconduct detailed by Disney/Pixar insiders. *The Hollywood Reporter*. Retrieved from https://www.hollywoodreporter.com/news/john-lasseters-pattern-alleged-misconduct-detailed-by-disney-pixar-insiders-1059594h

McNamara, M. (2019, February 26). Must reads: Emma Thompson's letter to Skydance: Why I can't work for John Lasseter. *Los Angeles Times*. Retrieved from https://www.latimes.com/entertainment/la-et-mn-emma-thompson-john-lasseter-skydance-20190226-story.html

Price, D. (2008). *The Pixar touch: The making of a company*. New York: Alfred A. Knopf.

Schellong, M. (2019, April 17). Pixar's SparkShorts set out to ignite more diversity in animation. *Delaware Public Media*. Retrieved from https://www.delawarepublic.org/post/pixars-sparkshorts-set-out-ignite-more-diversity-animation

Smolcic, C. (2018, June 27). How Pixar's open sexism ruined my dream job. *Variety*. Retrieved from https://variety.com/2018/film/news/pixar-boys-club-john-lasseter-cassandra-smolcic-1202858982/

Sørensen, J.B. (2002). The strength of corporate culture and the reliability of performance. *Administrative Science Quarterly, 47*(1), 70–91.

SparksShorts - Pixar artists' project. (2019, January 10). *Facebook*. Retrieved from https://www.facebook.com/Pixar/videos/1453347761465094/h

Stewart, J. (2006). *Disney war*. New York: Simon and Schuster.

Wasko, J. (2001). *Understanding Disney* (1st ed.). Malden, MA: Polity.

3 Marvel Heroes at Mouseketeer Prices

When Disney+ launched, the offerings under the "Disney" tab included the first five episodes of the original *The Mickey Mouse Club (MMC)* that debuted on October 3, 1955. These episodes give us a glimpse into a world that is at times incomprehensible. The first segment in the pilot episode is a "Mickey Mouse Club Newsreel," which begins with a montage of children from around the world, over which a narrator promises to give us "the news of the day for the leaders of tomorrow." That promise is punctuated with a shot of the Mouseketeers cheerfully waving to the camera as if to introduce themselves as among those leaders. The first clip of the newsreel shows two boys, wearing what appear to be Cub Scout uniforms, riding on an airboat in the Florida Everglades driven by Mike Osceola, whom we are told is the great-grandson of Chief Osceola of the Seminole tribe. The camera follows the boat through different parts of the Everglades, as the narrator tells us these are "secret passages no white man could follow." At the close of this segment, the narrator explains that Chief Osceola was "tricked into leaving the Everglades and died in prison. But now it's time to go." Apparently, this casual dismissal of a historical tragedy of injustice is what passed for multiculturalism in 1955.

In another segment in the same episode, entitled "What I want to be," actor Alvy Moore, who later played Hank Kimball on the television show *Green Acres* (1965), is introduced as a representative of The Mickey Mouse Club who claims to be looking for "special" children with an interest in a career in aviation. The scene is at an airport, and Moore approaches a young girl named Pat, who is on a school field trip. No one seems the least bit troubled by this strange man hanging out at the airport approaching children. In fact, Pat's teacher encourages Moore's efforts to help children plan for their careers, and Pat takes this strange man to meet a boy who is also interested in flying. At the risk of stating the obvious, it clearly was a different time.

While we might find these scenes problematic and even disturbing, audiences in 1955 apparently did not. *MMC* was a very successful show and has become a cultural institution. The show not only was for children, but it was also about them too. Most notably, the Mouseketeers featured young

DOI: 10.4324/9781003364658-3

people singing, dancing, and performing in the various staged skits for the show. Although there would be some adult Mouseketeers (Jimmie and Roy, for example), the focus was always on the children, and *MMC* has always been a showcase for exceptional young people. Over the years, and in its various manifestations, the Mouseketeers would introduce the talents of Annette Funicello, Keri Russell, Ryan Gosling, Justin Timberlake, Christina Aguilera, and Britney Spears, among many others.

This chapter is not so much about *MMC* as it is about how the Disney+ original program *Marvel's Hero Project* (*MHP*) reflects this iconic Disney show. Like *MMC*, *MHP* focuses on exceptional young people. This unscripted program is featured under the Marvel section of the service, and in each of its 20 episodes, we are introduced to a young person who has made a significant contribution to their community or has overcome a significant challenge. As the tagline for the show reads, *MHP* is about "real kids making a real difference." Admittedly, these 'kids' do not sing and dance or perform skits, but *MMC* is an important touchstone for the analysis of *MHP* because of the ways the latter parallels the former.

These parallels, we will maintain, are purposeful to the extent that they allow for practices of brand equity and serve to align the Marvel brand with the Disney brand. Despite the problematic content of the first episodes of *MMC*, the program (in all of its iterations) reflects the elements of the Classic Disney style, particularly the sense of innocence and optimism that permeate the shows. Marvel is a brand that was already fully formed before its acquisition by Disney (in sharp contrast to Pixar, which developed its brand under the influence of the Disney Company); therefore, its content does not always reflect these elements of style (Flanagan, McKenny & Livingstone, 2016). We offer up the ending of *Avengers: Infinity War* (2018) as a case in point. *MHP*, on the other hand, clearly reflects the elements of style associated with the Disney brand and provides important intertextual links between Marvel and Disney. Primary among those links are the parallels with *MMC*.

In this chapter, we will begin with a brief history of Marvel Comics, tracing Marvel Studios' emergence and the expansion of the Marvel Cinematic Universe after the Disney acquisition. We then provide some background on *MMC* and identify those points that will inform our analysis of *MHP*. We then analyze the first season of *MHP*, drawing points of connection between the Marvel and Disney brands and identifying the show's brand equity. We conclude, however, that these branding efforts are not necessarily equitable where these "real kids" are concerned.

The Rise of Marvel Studios

Marvel Comics was founded in 1939 as Timely Comics, but its brand did not really begin to emerge until 1961 when Stan Lee and Jack Kirby began developing the *Spider-Man* (1962) and *Fantastic Four* (1961) comics.

In fact, these were some of the first Marvel characters to make the jump to other media, with animated television shows appearing in 1967. These intellectual properties would be revived in animated shows broadcast on NBC in the 1970s and 1980s. In addition, Marvel began producing live-action adaptations of the Spider-Man and The Incredible Hulk characters, which would air on PBS and CBS, respectively. *Spidey Super Stories* (1974) was a recurring feature on *The Electric Company* (1971), while *The Incredible Hulk* (1978) was a primetime drama. Because the company began to be more involved in both animated and live production, Marvel was purchased by New World Entertainment in 1986. New World was an independent film production company founded by Roger Corman, but after experiencing financial difficulties, New World would sell off Marvel to Ron Perelman in 1989 (Raviv, 2004).

Perelman was infamous on Wall Street for raising capital on the junk bond market and for acquiring companies, then turning a profit by selling off parts of these companies and their assets. In other words, he often bought companies in order to dismantle them. Initially, it appeared that Perelman's purchase was a positive development for Marvel. The quality of Marvel's comic books improved, and the price was increased. In fact, after two years, Perelman and his management team had significantly increased Marvel's revenue and profits. Unfortunately, some questionable choices by Perelman followed this success. First, Perelman made a stock offering of Marvel that raised $82 million, little of which was reinvested into Marvel; instead, that money was invested in other companies Perelman owned and was used to pay down his debt (Bryant, 1998). By 1995 Marvel's stock had lost half its value and was heading toward bankruptcy. Perelman also fired one-third of Marvel's publishing office staff, and he was threatening to cease publication of Marvel comic books (Raviv, 2004).

While these plans were disturbing to Marvel's fan base, they threatened disaster for some of the companies that did business with Marvel. For example, Toy Biz was a company with an exclusive contract to produce Marvel action figures, a contract secured by giving up 46% of the company to Perelman. If Marvel ceased publishing, the value of those intellectual property rights (the characters) would significantly diminish. Therefore, Perelman's threat to close down Marvel posed an existential threat to Toy Biz as well. Mindful of this existential threat, the top partners of Toy Biz, Isaac Perlmutter and Avi Arad, approached Perelman with an idea: make movies based on Marvel comics (Raviv, 2004). Perlmutter and Arad believed that if the Marvel characters were spun off into films, it would open up a variety of ancillary markets and thereby increase the value of the intellectual property.

One of the sticking points in the efforts to turn Marvel into a film studio was the fact that the film rights for many of their superhero characters had already been sold off to other studios. After several very contentious legal battles, including the corporate bankruptcy, Marvel emerged with

Perlmutter and Arad positioned to pursue their idea and form Marvel Studios. The bankruptcy voided many of the previous film licensing contracts so that Marvel could negotiate new deals with film studios (Raviv, 2004). Those deals involved co-production of Marvel Studios films with other major studios such as Fox and Columbia.

As was the plan all along, Marvel Studios was also heavily involved in the ancillary product market. In fact, Perelman had planned to turn Marvel into a "little Disney," figuring the films could turn the superhero characters into lucrative intellectual property (Raviv, 2004). That plan came to its final fruition with the Disney acquisition but with limited participation by Arad and Perlmutter. Arad would leave Marvel in 2006 and was not with the company when the acquisition took place; Perlmutter stayed on at Marvel developing its film properties until those responsibilities were shifted to Kevin Feige.

Since the Disney acquisition, the performance of Marvel Studio films has been historic, particularly in the pre-pandemic period. For 2018, the two highest-grossing films were *Black Panther* (2018) and *Avengers: Infinity War,* with a combined box office revenue total of $1.3 billion. *Deadpool 2* (2018) and *Ant-Man and the Wasp* (2018) were also among the top ten grossing films for 2018 with $318 million and $216 million in box office receipts, respectively.[1] This was a significant improvement from the year before when Marvel characters only held the sixth (*Spider-Man: Homecoming*, 2017) and eighth (*Thor: Ragnarok*, 2017) place spots on the list of top-grossing films, but generally, the studio's track record has been solid. Under Disney, Marvel has also expanded its production significantly. The Marvel Cinematic Universe (MCU) began with films already in development, with distribution deals at other studios, including the first three films of the MCU, *Iron Man* (2008), *The Incredible Hulk* (2008), and *Iron Man 2* (2010). Disney has added several feature films and television shows to the Marvel franchise and many of those have been featured on Disney+.

Although Marvel no longer publishes annual financial reports as an independent company, and Disney does not break out the revenue generated by Marvel specifically, the success of Marvel's films in 2018 alone indicates the value of the acquisition. Tucked away in Disney's 2017 report is this passage about Marvel:

> Before the Company acquired Marvel in fiscal year 2010, Marvel had licensed the rights to third-party studios to produce and distribute feature films based on certain Marvel properties, including Spider-Man, The Fantastic Four, and X-Men. Under the licensing arrangements, the third-party studios incur the costs to produce and distribute the films, and the Company retains the merchandise licensing rights. Under the licensing arrangement for Spider-Man, the Company pays the third-party studio a licensing fee based on each film's box office receipts,

> subject to specified limits. Under the licensing arrangements for The Fantastic Four and X-Men, the third-party studio pays the Company a licensing fee and receives a share of the Company's merchandise revenue on these properties.
>
> (The Walt Disney Company, 2017, p. 11)

Therefore, almost seven years after the acquisition of Marvel, the value of the acquisition for Disney is still the intellectual property rights and the licensing fees.

Despite this success, Marvel Studios had already established its presence in the market before the Disney acquisition, as both a comic book publisher and a film studio. Disney's purchase of Marvel can be viewed as an acquisition of intellectual property, but we should recognize how its own media brand encompassed this property. As Martin Flanagan, Mike McKenny, and Andy Livingstone (2016) observe, the Marvel brand has waxed and waned through the years but has primarily signified a rebellious embrace of creativity. The brand voice for the company was established in a variety of practices designed to develop and engage the Marvel fan base. These included the "Bullpen Bulletin" and "Stan Lee's Soapbox," news and information pages within Marvel comics which Matthew Pustz has argued allowed Marvel to create "a participatory world for readers, a way of life for its true believers" (1999, p. 56). The attraction of this brand voice can be attributed to the fact that Marvel spoke with the "nonconformist voice of the 'hipster,'" and consequently, "Marvel began to seem rebellious at heart, more likely to challenge establishment values" (Flanagan, McKenny & Livingstone, 2016, House Style, para. 9).

In his analysis of Marvel's transition into film production, Derek Johnson argues that the nonconformist, rebellious nature of the brand was rearticulated in trade stories about the emergence of Marvel studios. He observes that these stories position Marvel as a creative force that stands in opposition to the established Hollywood studios:

> Moreover, in casting Hollywood as the villain and Marvel as the hero in the mythological terms of destiny that often structure comic book narratives . . . these trade stories reinforced Marvel's core comics expertise as a rationale for its growing "superpower" in a converged film industry.
>
> (Johnson, 2012, 21)

In other words, Marvel continued to draw on its brand identity as it positioned itself in contrast to the Hollywood establishment. Ironically, these trade stories culminated in the apotheosis of Marvel pursuing independent film production, which occurred shortly before they were taken over by Disney, one of the most well-established Hollywood studios.

Despite this acquisition, Flanagan, McKenny, and Livingstone argue that Marvel has successfully maintained its brand identity:

> It is important to attend to how Marvel has plotted and realized a transmedia storytelling strategy that maximizes industrial systems geared to convergence while (initially) shaping an image of itself as the most potently, independently creative new/old 'kid on the block' of popular Hollywood production. In this vein, its post-2009/Disney purchase story asks to be understood as consolidating an image of a radical yet proven (and thus, fiscally responsible) content producer; and, further, one that can strategically harmonize with the image and aims of its parent, The Walt Disney Company.
>
> (2016, All-New, para. 4)

We would maintain that with the launch of Disney+, asserting those brand harmonics was of utmost importance. Therefore, as original content was offered under both the Disney and Marvel labels, *MHP* needed to reflect those harmonics. We believe it does so by reflecting one of Disney's most iconic television shows, *MMC*. Yet, to bring that reflection into focus, we need to discuss elements of *MMC* which support our comparison.

The Club That's Made for You and Me

As we mentioned, *MMC* debuted on October 3, 1955, on the ABC network in a late afternoon time slot, allowing children to view the program after school. Walt Disney began shopping the show a few years earlier, with the primary purpose of raising money to support the Disneyland park. Although many different iterations of the show were discussed, Disney ultimately closed a $2.5 million deal with ABC to produce a daily one-hour show. This was not Disney's first television show because the company had produced specials and already had an anthology series, *The Disneyland Story* (1954), in production at ABC. In fact, Walt Disney felt overextended with overseeing the park and its related television show, so he delegated production of *MMC* to Bill Walsh. Walt, however, had very clear ideas about how the show should be produced, and he was particularly interested in the casting of the Mouseketeers. As Bill Cotter notes, "Walt wanted to avoid using known show business professionals, as he knew that the show had a better chance of success if audiences related to the Mouseketeers" (1997, p. 183). Therefore, the original cast included members who, while displaying talent, had little if any professional experience.

There were some exceptions, such as Lonnie Burr, who had already established a resume of television performances before joining *MMC*. Generally, however, the Mouseketeers were, by most standards, show business amateurs and were paid accordingly, earning the Screen Actors Guild minimum of $185 a week. When Burr and his mother, who managed his career and that of other clients, balked at this low pay, the show's producers threatened to ruin his career. As Burr relates, when his mother called Lee Traver, one of the casting agents, to decline the offer, "Traver told her that if I did not sign I would be black-balled and would 'never work in Hollywood again.' Her agency and all of her other clients would also become persona non grata, according to Traver" (Burr, 2014, p. 96). This aggressive tactic was in line with the larger strategy of keeping production costs low. After all, this was a show designed to make money to support Disneyland, and Walt knew that the cast of unknowns would work for the money offered (Cotter, 1997). While Burr was the exception in terms of his professional experience, he did not break the rule regarding talent compensation.

It is also important to note that the Mouseketeers primarily performed as themselves, with their real names emblazoned across their chests. True, they might dress in costumes for the various skits, but often when they sang and danced, they did so as themselves, clearly identified as Annette, Darlene, Bobby, and so on. As Burr observes, this approach was unique at the time. It allowed for the children viewing at home to identify with the Mouseketeers as Walt predicted. In addition, the Mouseketeers served as brand ambassadors for Disney, as they "were now identifiable kids who linked together with Mickey Mouse and the entire world of Walt Disney. Other shows at the time only had real kids in the 'peanut gallery'" (Burr, 2014, p. 91). Part of their ambassadorship was the required iconic mouse ears hat. As Bobby Burgess (2014) notes in his autobiography, the boy Mouseketeers were resistant to wearing these hats, and if they were lost, the studio would charge the negligent Mouseketeer $50 for a replacement. At this point, we should note that the mouse ears hats required the Mouseketeers to literally embody the Disney brand and assume the financial burden of maintaining that brand identity.

However, the use of unseasoned performers also had a downside, one that became quickly apparent in the production of a one-hour daily show. Originally 28 Mouseketeers were hired, but in order to accommodate the educational requirements, the Mouseketeers were split into "Red," "White," and "Blue" teams. The producers put the more talented members into the Red team, and this team took on most of the performance responsibilities, relegating the members of the other teams to what Burr might describe as "the peanut gallery." For example, Mary Espinosa, who along with Dickie Dodd was one of two Latinx cast members on the first season, appears in the second episode of the show only to serve as an audience member for the day's guest – balloon sculptor, prop comic, and (as we are told) Disneyland performer, Wally Boag. She is not even included in the Mouseketeer roll call for the episode. Not only was Espinosa relegated to this minor supporting role (her IMDB.com profile only lists appearances in three episodes), she was not offered a contract for the second season. In other words, although the Mouseketeers were supposed to represent "real kids," they also need to be exceptional performers, and ultimately, they also needed to be white.

Funicello, as an Italian-American, would be as close to a diverse cast member as would appear in the rest of the original series. In ways, although perhaps not intentionally, the *MMC* was an early template for the reality talent show competition, as the Mouseketeers performed as themselves, and the less talented members were shunted off to the "peanut gallery" and then dropped from the show.

The production demands of the series would also require a regimented schedule and segmented shows. Each of the five days the show was broadcast would have a particular theme: Monday was "Fun with Music Day," Tuesday was "Guest Star Day," Wednesday was "Anything Can Happen Day," Thursday was "Circus Day," and Friday was "Talent Round-up Day" (Cotter, 1997). Within this scheduling regimen, the episodes themselves had four standing segments. The first segment was usually devoted to "The Mickey Mouse Club Newsreel," where the accomplishments of exceptional children from various locales were covered as news events. The segment referenced at the beginning of the chapter is an example, and other segments showcased young people who excelled at speedboat racing, rodeo competitions or were the recipients of Future Farmers of America awards. The second segment usually focused on the daily theme and involved a performance by the Mouseketeers, including their roll call. The third segment would feature a serialized story, such as *The Adventures of Spin and Marty* (1955), and later Funicello would have her own self-titled serial. The fourth and final segment featured one of the old Disney cartoons, which reflected a very cost-effective practice of repurposing back catalog titles, which is still present today. In fact, the presence of *MMC* on Disney+ is a case in point. With this schedule and these segments in place, the producers could more easily decide how to fill five hours of programming each week.

The plan worked. *MMC* was an immediate success and had achieved a 52.9% share by the airing of its fourth episode. The ratings following the first season had included over 14 million viewers, with one-third of those being adults (Cotter, 1997). To put those numbers in perspective, there were only 30 million households with a television in 1955, so the ratings were significant for the period (Number of TV Households in America 1950–1978, n.d.). The show's success was also evident in the fan mail the cast would receive and the fan clubs that emerged for certain cast members, including Annette and Lonnie (Burr, 2014). Yet, perhaps the most lucrative indication of the show's success was the merchandise the show sold. As Jennifer Armstrong notes:

> Mouseketeer hats (retail price: 69 cents) became the Disney empire's best-selling item over the next several years, peaking at twenty-four thousand a day. Bubble-bath sets, "Mousegetars," Mouseketeer dolls, and more than two hundred other kinds of merchandise helped fulfill fan's insatiable need for *Mickey Mouse Club* gear.
>
> (2010, p. 45)

Extrapolating from these numbers, the associated merchandise generated tens of thousands of dollars daily for the Disney Company at a time when the dollar had almost ten times the value it has today.

The success of the show's merchandising further illustrates how well the Mouseketeers operated as brand ambassadors. These "real kids," performing as themselves, were both relatable and aspirational for their fans, and those aspirations could be realized, at least materially, through the various products. This merchandise was promoted on the show and also reflected the purpose of supporting Disneyland. For example, on the fifth episode, a "Talent Round-Up Day," a young trumpeter, Larry Ashurst, is inducted as an "honorary Mouseketeer," and in addition to his mouse ears, he received a "whole strongbox of mouseketreasures." Annette and Bobbie open the strongbox at the end of the episode to reveal a "Frontierland Indian Brave Outfit," a "Frontierland Frontiersman Double Holster and Pistol Set," a "Disneyland Steamboat Captain Outfit," and a "Chief Engineer Disneyland RR Outfit." As we mentioned earlier, like the program itself, even the merchandise reflected the casual racism of 1955. More to the point, this strongbox closed the promotional loop that connected the Mouseketeers to the merchandise, the Disneyland Park, and finally, the Disney brand.

Given the success of the merchandise and *MMC*, Disney was able to draw a high value from the Mouseketeers at a very low cost. As noted, the cast was hired at scale, and although their contracts allowed for a percentage of the gross of merchandise, as Burr explains:

> Our 2.5% of GROSS (sic) versus the ADJUSTED (sic) net on merchandising was paid out in a few, tiny increments during the '50s, but nothing has been paid since then. . . The MMC and Mouseketeer products and new ones that were introduced since the '50s and will continue into perpetuity if they make money are sold with no monies going to the Mouseketeers.
>
> (Burr, 2014, p. 67)

Even the most successful member of the original Mouseketeers, Annette Funicello, had to sue to have her pay increased and was still under contract with Disney when she began her series of Beach Party films. Indicative of how aware Walt was of Annette's value to the Disney brand; he forbade her from wearing a bikini when he agreed to loan her out for the films.

At this point, it should be clear how *MMC* reflected elements of the Classic Disney style. Even in the first five episodes streaming on Disney+, it is clear that the show was designed as light entertainment, offering musical acts and plenty of slapstick humor. The representation of both gender and ethnicity was not only stereotypical, but by today's standards, also highly offensive. Still, the show projected a sense of optimism and innocence epitomized by the Mouseketeers. After all, they, along with the other kids who appeared in the opening newsreel, were the "leaders of tomorrow." The

Mouseketeers may have been represented as "real kids," but they were also exceptional; therefore, our future was in good hands.

As we will demonstrate in the next section, *MHP* also represents elements of the Classic Disney style, but in addition, we have found notable and significant parallels between the series and *MMC*. Our argument here is not that *MHP* is a version of *MMC* (there are already plenty of versions of that show); instead, we will maintain that the production of *MHP* is informed by practices that were established during the making of *MMC*.

Branding the Heroes

Like *MMC*, *MHP* has a clear and consistent structure, as we will use the pilot episode to illustrate. Admittedly, the segmentation of the show is not the most important parallel between the two shows, and this similar segmentation can be found in other unscripted television shows. Yet, by discussing these segments, we can recreate the show's text in an organized manner and thereby identify some of the other parallels.

In the show's introduction, we are shown Marvel characters being sketched out and then realized on the actual comic book page, while a narrative voice-over tells us:

> At Marvel, our stories and our superheroes are inspired by real-life heroes. So, the editors of some of our best-known comics have come together to work on a particular project; to find and tell the stories of kids doing the extraordinary. Helping communities near and far and changing the world are the kids who inspire our stories for years to come.

Implied in this introduction is the fact that these heroes, like the Mouseketeers, will prove to be future leaders in that their stories will inspire us "for years to come."

In the first episode, we are then introduced to Jordan, who remarks, "this small idea has grown into like this humongous thing." Jordan, we later learn, was born missing a hand, and her title slide includes the phrase: "Limb Differences."[2] We are shown the prosthetic arm that Jordan has designed that also functions as a glitter gun, and she remarks, "this arm gives me so much confidence because I made this, and I can use what I made to help a lot of other kids." The narrator adds, "Jordan is already a hero. Now, we bring her story to the world . . . making her a Marvel Superhero, immortalized in her very own comic as a member of Marvel's Hero Project."

Surprisingly, the introduction does not end there. Now the video shifts to animated images framed as comic book panels that show kids involved in various actions. Over these images, the narrator continues: "They're everyday kids, who have accomplished the amazing. Now, their true stories will reveal the heroes that live among us. This is Marvel Hero Project." And in case the viewer missed any of that, this narration appears in text boxes in the animation, keeping in line with the comic book aesthetic.

After this introductory segment, the scene shifts to New York City and Marvel headquarters' offices for an "Editorial Meeting Brainstorm for Jordan's Comic" (this explanation is rendered in a text box as well). In this meeting, we are introduced to Sana Amana, "VP, Content & Character," Stephen Wacker, "VP, Creative & Content," Sarah Amos, "VP, Development," and Nick Lowe, "VP, Executive Editor." The discussion revolves around Jordan and why she is a superhero; the editing in this segment continues with the comic book panel aesthetic and the text boxes. In this discussion, Jordan is identified as a hero by Sana because "she is owning the fact that she is different and finding a lot of joy in it." Stephen adds that Jordan has "taken it to another level in her inventions. . . to turn herself into sort of a superhero." Sarah elaborates by suggesting that Jordan's perspective on design is informed by her unique perspective, one that Nick compares to a "Wakandian point of view" and the Marvel character Shuri, references to the very popular *Black Panther.* Sana then summarizes the discussion by noting, "Jordan is encouraging people who are coming from the same background as she is and saying, 'if we can include them as designers and engineers, then what a different world it will be'." In this segment, clear lines of connection are drawn between Jordan and the Marvel Universe.

After this segment, the scene shifts to Jordan performing as a cheerleader. Jordan explains how the experience of cheerleading has improved her confidence and that the visibility is a way of "getting people to know limb differences." She continues: "The fact that I have a difference is so cool, and I can use it for so many cool things. I'm still working on doing so much more." During Jordan's voice-over, we are shown footage that displays her limb difference. Jordan's mother then relates her reaction when Jordan was born, and how after her initial shock, she and her husband immediately recognized that Jordan "was fine." In other words, they accepted Jordan's limb difference at her birth. As her father explains, Jordan did not need much help, and she has played sports and has "done everything along the way." Jordan concurs and observes that she was very stubborn and wanted to learn and do things on her own. Her mother points out that Jordan was "congenitally forced to be a problem solver," and as Jordan explains, she just had to learn to do things "a bit differently from everyone else." Therefore, within the first few minutes of the episode, we are provided a perspective on limb difference that is not only supportive but productive. In other words, Jordan's difference is also her creative inspiration.

Despite this optimistic view of limb differences, the episode does not ignore problems of social stigma. As Jordan relates, "It gets annoying when people look." An off-camera producer asks her, "what's the look that people give?" She demonstrates with a nervous side-eye glance. In addition, Jordan's mother later notes that people with disabilities are often not fully employed. Yet, Jordan avers that "it is good to be different," and this is a sentiment that is expressed several times during the episode, and not just by Jordan, but by her siblings and her friends.

Jordan's difference, however, is also represented as a unique perspective that fuels her creativity. When she was ten, she was invited to participate in a design workshop that challenged her to build on her difference. A video of Jordan at the workshop shows her demonstrating a device she had built that replaced her missing hand and expelled glitter. We are then shown footage of Jordan developing and refining her design. As she notes, "by me growing up having to figure out things in a different way than everyone else has given me the design thinking and maker thoughts." Therefore, Jordan views her limb difference as the inspiration for her designs, an extension of her ability to solve problems posed by her difference.

Ultimately, Jordan designs a glitter gun that fits over her arm, replacing her missing hand, an object she has named "The Unicorn Project." Jordan is then shown pitching her design and demonstrating the project to *The Shark Tank* (2009) cast on the *Rachael Ray Show* (2006). As she observes, "People with two hands can't shoot glitter out of their arm. Might as well take your difference and make something really cool that shares the joy of differences." Jordan then demonstrates the refined Unicorn Project for a TEDx talk, during which she tells the audience, "use your differences for good, because your differences are amazing, and you never know what amazing things you can do with them." Jordan's mother concurs and offers that Jordan's TEDx talk "was a moment of showing that disability is an opportunity," and clearly, that is the message we as an audience are meant to receive.

Indeed, Jordan later claims that her difference imparts an ability to teach people, and with this statement, we are positioned as her students. However, this statement also operates as a segue to a segment that shows Jordan leading workshops "to let people who are disabled build off of their disability." As one of the young participants of the workshop notes, "I want to change the world, create something that I think is good for me, and then other people can do it for themselves, and it will just keep going on and on." Ultimately, Jordan believes that training others to incorporate accessibility into design thinking can lead to products that more people can easily use and potentially open new job prospects for those who incorporate difference into their designs. Jordan's message, and the message of this pilot episode, is inherently optimistic: difference is an opportunity, an opportunity for all of us.

The third, and relatively brief, segment of the episode, returns to Marvel's headquarters, where Wacker and Lowe discuss the design of Jordan's comic book. Wacker observes that the comic has focused "on the fact, that as she is, the way she was born, she was a hero." We are shown the comic book panels in various stages of completion, and Lowe notes how the panels show Jordan reaching out to other people and developing her designs in a lab. They both agree that her inventiveness is her superpower, so the cover features Jordan with her Unicorn Project, rendered in her favorite color (purple). We are shown how the cover is constructed, and the color added. Wacker then notes that Jordan will receive her comic at an event attended by both her father and her brother ("usually she just travels with her mother").

For the fourth and final segment of the pilot, the scene shifts again, this time to the Cambridge Science Festival at MIT. At this event, Jordan's mother is invited to the stage. She reads a letter contained in an envelope emblazoned with the Marvel logo (we also see the letter has been printed on Marvel letterhead):

> Your friends at Marvel have something amazing to tell you. You have dedicated yourself to helping people navigate how difficult it can be when you are unlike everyone else. Your devotion to making the world a more inclusive place inspires us . . . and that's what makes you a superhero. Jordan, because you strive to change the global conversation about people with disabilities, we believe you represent everything that Marvel stands for.

Jordan is then presented with a box, again the Marvel logo is visible, and inside she finds a jacket: "just like the classic X-Men uniforms, this jacket will serve as an unmistakable symbol of your membership in the elite Marvel Hero Project." The letter also indicates that Marvel is making a "Tony Stark sized donation in your honor to an organization that supports kids with limb difference in the amount of $10,000." Finally, Jordan is presented with the comic book portraying her as a Marvel superhero.

Jordan's excitement is palpable in this segment, as is the excitement of her friends and family who have attended the event. They are shown reading the comic book and commenting on how it reflects Jordan. As her brother remarks:

> It is kind of surreal seeing your family member in the same style that you see, like, Spider-Man, Iron Man, Captain America, Captain Marvel . . . My sister is a superhero. She already was, but now we have proof.

The segment then cuts to a camera pan of a wall of comic books, much like the displays in a comic book store. Jordan's comic book is then slipped into a plastic cover alongside an *Avengers* comic. Then the camera pulls out to reveal Jordan's book among a wall of comic books from the Marvel universe, to display proof that she is indeed a superhero within that universe.

All 20 episodes of *MHP* follow this basic structure. Each episode is devoted to a different young person who is introduced in the beginning segment. The Marvel staff then discusses their accomplishments (although different staff members contribute to these discussions in the various episodes). The young person featured is compared to a Marvel character. Their accomplishments are then chronicled in the third segment. They are awarded the Marvel jacket and comic in the final segment, along with the check for $10,000.

The optimism in the pilot episode is continued in the other episodes, and the young people featured often reflect diversity and difference. The third episode features "Unstoppable Adonis," a blind high school student who plays for his school's football team. The fifth episode features "Mighty Rebekah," a young transgender advocate for LGBTQ rights. In the "Battlin' Braden" episode, we are introduced to Braden, whose empathy with other hearing-impaired youth inspires him to raise money to supply hearing aids to those that cannot afford them. Other episodes focus on young people who have committed themselves to help others. "Make Way for Jahkil" focuses on the efforts of Jahkil to provide essential personal care products for the homeless. "Soaring Seamus" portrays the work of a young rock climber who is raising scholarship money for the families of veterans. Each "hero" in each episode is shown to be successful in their efforts to accomplish their goals and help others.

Although a sense of optimism dominates, the portrayals of these young people do not overlook the difficulties some of them face. For example, Rebekah's father, who is a pastor of a Lutheran church, remarks on his daughter's gender transition: "it is difficult to work through the emotional pieces of it . . . the scariness . . . the worry about what else this is going to mean." Later in the episode, he elaborates on that worry: "I worry who's going to know and how they are going to react. I worry someone is not going to understand who she is and hurt her." His comments are perhaps informed by the data that demonstrates transgender people are not only subject to violence, but that victimization can occur early in their lives and can occur multiple times (Stotzer, 2009). His wife, and Rebekah's mother, shares her own concern:

> The statistics are terrifying. The biggest one for the parents of trans kids, and we were faced with it right away, is that 41% of transgendered people attempt suicide at some point in their life, 41%. And what we know is that support is the single most mitigating factor in that.

Therefore, this episode of the series does not overlook the conditions that transgender people face, but these conditions render Rebekah's efforts even more heroic. In addition, it is quite clear that despite their concerns, Rebekah's parents support her unequivocally, and Rebekah's mission is to extend that support to other transgender kids and their families. Indeed, the Marvel staff equate Rebekah's mission to her superpower and her bravery. Ultimately, Rebekah's story, too, is one of optimism.

Obviously then, *MHP* does not reflect the Classic Disney style where gender is concerned. We would add that the series is also very inclusive where ethnicity is concerned (nine of the episodes introduce us to heroes of color). Still, the series conveys a sense of optimism in ways that reflect other elements of Disney style. For example, the innocence of youth is often displayed in a subtextual way through the optimism of these heroes; the young people firmly believe they can ease the problems they confront. Their heroism reflects a sense of individualism because they are depicted as taking action and making a difference through their own initiative. That initiative also displays a strong work ethic; for example, Jahkil is shown personally preparing the essential product bags for the homeless. In other episodes, we are shown "Dynamic Daniella" helping to build housing in Mexico, and "High-Kickin' Izzy," who overcame her arthrogryposis (a crippling condition of the joints and muscles) to win several world championships in Taekwondo. Finally, given that these heroes are represented as "everyday kids," they are framed as reflecting mainstream America.

As we have mentioned, although the segmentation of *MHP* reflects that of *MMC*, this similarity can be found in other forms of television and the genre of reality television in particular. Although reality television is a distinct genre, there are also many subgenres (Huff, 2006). Although the segments found in *MHP* resemble the segments found in the makeover and renovation subgenres, the show has much more in common with *MMC* than many of the offerings in these reality television subgenres.

For example, both *MMC* and *MHP* focus on extraordinary young people but offer them as exemplars of "real kids." Indeed, in both shows, the real identity of the young people (their names) is front and center; literally, on the uniforms of the Mouseketeers with their names emblazoned on their chests, and so too the episodes of *MHP* are also named after the heroes represented. In addition, the young people on both shows embody the brands of the show's producers. In the case of *MMC*, the mouse ears hat represents this embodied branding; for *MHP*, the heroes embody the brand the moment they don their jackets. While MHP participants value these jackets (like Jordan, their excitement is palpable), and they do not seem to have the disdain that some of the Mouseketeers had for their hats, the textual effect is the same. In other words, like those hats, the Marvel jacket turns the heroes into brand ambassadors, to the degree that they now visibly represent the Marvel brand. The presentation of these jackets (and their comic books) to *MHP* participants also closely resembles how "honorary Mouseketeers" on *MMC* were inducted into the show's Mickey Mouse Club when they too were presented with a box of branded products. Yet one of the most significant similarities relates to the production practices of both shows, and the way Disney treated and compensated this young talent.

Have Your Parents Sign Here and Initial Here

A closer look at the fine print in the comic books prepared for the members of *MHP* reveals another essential aspect of the production practices.

A text box at the conclusion of each comic contains the standard copyright information and this language: "All characters featured in this issue and the distinctive names and likenesses thereof, and all related indicia are trademarks of Marvel Characters Inc." This language is unequivocal; when a hero is inducted, their identities (as rendered in the book) become licensed intellectual property of Marvel, and in turn, Disney. In addition, the show itself is copyrighted by Marvel, and it resides on a streaming service that also carries the Disney copyright.

The life story rights of these heroes would need to be secured in the production process. Given that the show's heroes are all minors, the contracts for those rights would have been signed and approved by the parents. Although the actual contracts secured for the production are not readily available to the public (this is Disney, after all), the terms of these contracts often include protection of the producers from liability and defamation suits. In addition, those contracts often secure the cooperation of the person depicted and/or their family, the rights to publicity, and access to personal documents, including photos and videos. Given that the episodes in the series feature the families of the heroes and often their pictures and home videos, the actual contracts signed by the parents of the heroes most likely reflect these general practices (Litwak, 2017). In any event, the final products of *MHP* are contingent on those heroes allowing Marvel to secure the rights to their likeness and their life stories, all of which become intellectual property for the Disney corporation.

For this show, Disney receives some very compelling life stories. The reviews *MHP* received indicate those stories found an appreciative audience, with a 92% Tomatometer score on *Rotten Tomatoes* and an 86% audience score. *Common Sense Media* gave the show five stars and marked it as an approved selection for families (Camacho, 2019). Bonnie Burton, writing for *C|NET*, summarized her review this way:

> While Marvel's Hero Project doesn't include the kind of superheroes we're used to seeing battle bad guys on the big screen, the series could motivate both kids and adults struggling with problems in their lives and communities to start working toward solutions. Acting locally to help improve the lives of others – whether it be cleaning up a park, helping deliver meals to the homeless, or showing kids they can do anything regardless of disabilities – is the kind of heroism we could all use right about now.
>
> (2019, para. 20, 21)

We agree. We, too, find the stories of these new Marvel heroes to be compelling, and we must acknowledge the high level of production values contained in the program. These stories are told in a very respectful way, of the young people involved and the issues they have embraced. As other media scholars have noted (Sperb, 2018), it can be challenging to offer criticism of

Disney's content. We face a similar challenge when confronted with *MHP*, in that our observations may be construed as disrespectful of the heroes represented in the episodes. On the contrary, we believe that these extraordinary young people are worthy of the honors they receive from Marvel and actually are worth more than they are given.

While unscripted television proved popular with audiences, the genre also became popular with producers, but for economic reasons. Simply put, these shows are cheap to produce, and one of the areas in which costs are contained is talent compensation. While talent compensation for a long-running scripted show can cost multiple millions of dollars per episode, unscripted shows generally pay their talent a lot less, with some notable exceptions. In addition, there is a critical distinction in unscripted production between talent, who might appear in every episode or serve as a host for the show, and participants (those who only appear in one episode or only appear in a limited number of episodes). As Paul Battista and Hayley Hughes note, "(p)articipants basically have no leverage in the negotiation process, and they are required to sign a lengthy 'participant agreement' in which they consent to give the producers many wide-ranging rights" (2016, p. 14). It is most likely that the *Marvel's Hero Project* heroes and their families would be required to sign similar types of agreements.

While these heroes and their families may receive compensation for their participation, it is likely that any compensation was minimal. For unscripted shows, compensation can vary widely, but the vast majority of people who appear on these shows are only paid a daily rate of $20 to $30 plus expenses (Nededog, 2016). As Yomi Adegoke (2020) reported for *The Guardian*, streaming services like Netflix and Hulu eschew compensation for their docuseries programs because of concerns about credibility. She notes the example of Hulu's *Fyre Fraud* (2019) documentary, which drew criticism when it was revealed that the central figure of the film, Billy McFarland, was paid to participate. Where these types of programs are concerned, it is one of the rare moments where the interest in credibility aligns with production interests. In other words, providing minimum compensation for the participants (or forgoing compensation altogether) improves the bottom line. Again, the specific compensation offered by the producers of *MHP* is not public information. There is, however, no compelling evidence that the show deviated from the standard practices of unscripted television production. Therefore, we can only draw conclusions from what we know.

Here is what we know. These Marvel heroes receive a branded jacket, a comic book that is copyrighted as intellectual property, and a $10,000 donation made to a charity in their honor. In addition, we should also note that this donation is most likely deducted from corporate taxes, thereby increasing the value of the compensation for Marvel. Marvel, in turn, receives the brand equity of these heroes' stories and the goodwill that comes from the association with their remarkable accomplishments. In addition, Marvel can create programming that conveys the values of the Classic

Disney style and reproduces some important aspects of an iconic Disney program, especially in regard to talent compensation. In other words, *MHP* offers original content that allows the Marvel brand to fit nicely under the Disney+ label, and like *MMC* before it, the show can deliver that brand equity at minimal costs.

To put this in perspective, at $10,000 per episode, the first season of *MHP* cost the company $200,000 in charitable donations. As a point of comparison, when Emily Maynard appeared on ABC's (another Disney company) *The Bachelorette* (2003), it is reported that she received $250,000 (Bricker, 2018). For another point of comparison, when Bob Chapek took over as Disney CEO, his compensation included a $15 million annual incentive grant (Parker, 2020). In other words, these Marvel heroes receive a fraction of this compensation, and if Marvel had increased the donation to $100,000 for each episode, and Chapek made up this difference through his incentive grant, he still would have received $13 million.

Given that these extraordinary young people have allowed their likenesses and life stories to become intellectual property for Marvel and Disney, they have provided a great deal of value given that they have become brand ambassadors for these companies. In addition, they have also contributed to programming that was important to the launch of the Disney+ service. We agree with both Marvel and Disney; these young people are true heroes. We just believe they are worth a lot more.

We believe this is especially true given what the show delivered for Disney. As we mentioned, *MHP* parallels *MMC*. It provided a segmented program, focused on extraordinary "everyday" young people, it turned them into brand ambassadors who embodied the brand, and it served to promote the licensed merchandise. And all of this was delivered in a lovely branded box. The essential function of this branding was to provide a program that linked Marvel's rebellious identity with Disney's propagation of innocence, optimism, and individualism. In fact, *MHP* illustrates that these brands were not all that different after all. The Classic Disney style easily contains the rebellious nature of Marvel.

While Disney was able to deploy the Marvel band successfully with *MHP*, at least where the critical reviews are concerned, there is little indication the series brought much else to the service. Disney does not release much data about its Disney+ original programming. Therefore, there is little information about how many viewers *MHP* actually attracted. One indication, and it is telling, is that well over two years after it debuted, there are still no plans for a second season. In other words, brand equity may be the most significant benefit the show offers Disney, but it also provided Disney with very affordable content for the launch of the Disney+ service. Yet even the economics of the production does not seem to justify another season. As a point of contrast, another show which also debuted on Disney+, *The Mandalorian*, has already aired its second season, and at the time of this writing, the release of a third season is planned as well. *The Mandalorian*, however, was ranked by Nielsen as the most-watched streaming series for the week of December 14–20 (Clark, 2021). More on that series in the next chapter.

Although it did not prove to be as successful as *The Mandalorian*, *MHP* did its duty where the Marvel and Disney brands were concerned. The young people depicted were heroes in that they challenged accepted ideas about a variety of identities and issues, and their actions support the idea that Marvel sides with the rebels. Yet, their actions also reflect the innocence and optimism that have been important elements of the Disney brand. Granted, *MHP* has not received a second season, and it is clear that Disney is using Disney+ to extend the Marvel Cinematic Universe with other shows like *WandaVision*, *The Falcon and the Winter Soldier* (2021) and *Loki*. Still, for a studio that has built its brand by featuring the talents of young people, *MHP* continued that practice down to the very details of production. Finally, *MHP* delivered brand equity at minimal costs; no doubt, Walt would approve.

Notes

1 Box office information obtained from Boxofficemojo.com.
2 Throughout the episode, this term is used interchangeably with the word "disability," and although that interchangeable use may be problematic, it is what we found in the text.

References

Adegoke, Y. (2020, June 3). 'Netflix made all the money': who gets paid for our favorite TV show? *The Guardian*. Retrieved from https://www.theguardian.com/tv-and-radio/2020/jun/03/netflix-made-all-the-money-who-gets-paid-for-our-favourite-tv-shows

Armstrong, J. (2010). *Why? Because we still like you*. New York: Grand Central Publishing.

Battista, P., & Hughes, H. (2016). *Reality television contracts: How to negotiate the best deal*. New York: Allworth Press.

Bricker, T. (2018, October 11). How much reality TV contestants make (if anything). *E Online*. Retrieved from https://www.eonline.com/news/975767/how-much-reality-tv-contestants-actually-make-if-anything

Bryant, A. (1998, May 24). Pow! The punches that left Marvel reeling. *The New York Times*. Retrieved from https://www.nytimes.com/1998/05/24/business/pow-the-punches-that-left-marvel-reeling.html

Burgess, B. (2014). *Ears and bubbles: Dancing my way from The Mickey Mouse Club to the Lawrence Welk Show*. New York: Theme Park Press.

Burr, L. (2014). *The accidental Mouseketeer: Before and after The Mickey Mouse Club*. New York: Theme Park Press.

Burton, B. (2019, November 11). Disney Plus show Marvel Hero Project spotlights real-life superheroes. *CNET*. Retrieved from https://www.cnet.com/news/disney-plus-show-marvels-hero-project-spotlights-real-life-superheroes/

Camacho, M. (2019). Marvel's Hero Project. *Common Sense Media.* Retrieved from https://www.commonsensemedia.org/tv-reviews/marvels-hero-project

Clark, T. (2021, Jan. 14). 'The Mandalorian' finally beat 'The Office' as the most watched streaming series in the US, according to Nielsen. *Insider.* Retrieved from https://www.businessinsider.com/mandalorian-tops-nielsen-list-of-most-watched-streaming-tv-shows-2021-1

Cotter, B. (1997). *The Wonderful world of Disney television: A complete history.* New York: Hyperion.

Flanagan, M., McKenny, M., & Livingstone, A. (2016). *The Marvel Studios phenomenon: Inside a transmedia universe* [Kindle edition]. New York: Bloomsbury. Retrieved from https://www.amazon.com/Marvel-Studios-Phenomenon-Transmedia-Universe-ebook/dp/B01DLR71LO/ref=sr_1_1?crid=1SPZ0IMQ0ZVLY&keywords=The+Marvel+Studios+phenomenon%3A+Inside+a+transmedia+universe&qid=1661187325&sprefix=the+marvel+studios+phenomenon+inside+a+transmedia+universe+%2Caps%2C93&sr=8-1

Huff, R. (2006). *Reality television.* Westport, CT: Praeger Publishers.

Johnson, D. (2012). Cinematic destiny: Marvel Studios and the trade stories of industrial convergence. *Cinema Journal, 52*(1), 1–24.

Litwak, M. (2017). *Dealmaking in the film and television Industry: From negotiations to final contract* (4th ed.). Los Angeles: Silman-James Press.

Nededog, J. (2016, June 7). Here's how reality TV shows get away with paying people nothing. *Business Insider.* Retrieved from https://www.businessinsider.com/reality-tv-shows-pay-nothing-2016-6http://www.fundinguniverse.com/company-histories/netflix-inc-history/

Number of TV Households in America 1950–1978. (n.d.). *The American Century.* Retrieved from https://americancentury.omeka.wlu.edu/items/show/136

Parker, R. (2020, March 30). Bob Iger to forgo Disney salary, top execs to take pay cuts amid virus crisis. *The Hollywood Reporter.* Retrieved from https://www.hollywoodreporter.com/news/bob-iger-forgo-disney-salary-top-execs-take-pay-cuts-1287418

Pustz, M. (1999). *Comic book culture, Fanboys and the true believers.* Jackson, MS: University Press of Mississippi.

Raviv, D. (2004). *Comic wars: Marvel's battle for survival.* New York: Marvel Comics.

Sperb, J. (2018). How (not) to teach Disney. *Journal of Film and Video, 70*(1), 47–60.

Stotzer, R. (2009). Violence against transgendered people: A review of United States data. *Aggression and Violent Behavior, 14*(3), 170–179.

The Walt Disney Company. (2017). *Fiscal Year 2017 Annual Financial Report.* Retrieved from https://thewaltdisneycompany.com/app/uploads/2017-Annual-Report.pdf

4 *The Mandalorian*

Disney's "Baby" Steps Toward Fan Service

When Disney acquired Lucasfilm in 2012, it was arguably the logical conclusion to a relationship that had been ongoing for decades. To put the relationship between Disney, George Lucas, and the *Star Wars* franchise into perspective, we should start at the beginning, when *Star Wars: Episode IV – A New Hope* first premiered in theaters in May of 1977. The film was a hit, and one that began the first trilogy of the franchise, suggestively numbered "Episode IV" to indicate that there were other episodes (read films) to be had (and to be made). Indeed, in 1980 *Star Wars: Episode V – The Empire Strikes Back* was released, followed by *Star Wars: Episode VI – Return of the Jedi* in 1983. The success of these sequels is also well established, but it is important to note how this initial trilogy inspired a massive amount of merchandise. In an interview with *Deadline*, Tom Pollock, former Universal Pictures CEO, recounts his experience as George Lucas' lawyer during negotiations of the Star Wars contracts with Fox (Fleming, 2020). According to Pollock, Lucas was intent on retaining the sequel rights to the *Star Wars* films and negotiated a smaller salary in order to retain those rights. After the first film became a hit, Lucas was able to negotiate a deal with Fox in which he would self-finance the sequel, while 20th Century Fox would have distribution and home video rights. However, the merchandising rights would revert to Lucas for the sequels, although Fox maintained them for *A New Hope*.

This deal is often held up as one of the savviest decisions in modern film history and spurred other studios to promote film merchandise aggressively. Undoubtedly, the merchandise deal also helped finance the expansion of the Lucasfilm empire, including the Skywalker Ranch compound and Industrial Light and Magic. Arguably the only studio with a more successful record in merchandising at the time was Disney, although their fortunes were in decline. The 1970s and 1980s are generally recognized as a prolonged slump for Disney (Russell, 2012). This slump is often attributed to less than inspired content (Andrews, 2019) and shifts in animation style and technology (Hahn, 2009). More importantly, Disney's failures during this period began to erode its brand identity with its core audience. Indeed,

 DOI: 10.4324/9781003364658-4

Lucas himself noted that, during this period, Disney had "abdicated" its throne as the leader in content for children (Biskind, 1998).

The use of the word "abdicated" is interesting because it suggests voluntary, purposeful abandonment. Certainly, Disney did not set out to alienate children and family audiences during the 1970s and 1980s. However, with a focus on live-action fare including everything from Western-themed comedies involving aging comedians from television shows (*The Apple Dumpling Gang*, 1975), to a body switch science fiction fable featuring Jodie Foster and Barbara Harris (*Freaky Friday,* 1976), the 1970s indeed showed Disney falling victim to some mission creep. In addition, there is Disney's attempt to capitalize on the success of *Star Wars* with the dark sci-fi fare of *The Black Hole* (1979), the Faustian themed *The Devil and Max Devlin* (1981), the technocentric *Tron* (1982), and even the harrowing imagery found in some key scenes in the animated and supposedly child friendly *The Fox and the Hound* (1981). Today, we might say Disney got off-brand in the 1970s and 1980s. For whatever combination of reasons, Disney had indeed (as Lucas noted) strayed from its path as the leader in films geared toward children and families.

This opened the door for *Star Wars* to obtain a significant footprint in a market previously dominated by Disney. George Lucas said of *Star Wars*, "this is a Disney movie" (Lambie, 2019), and even laid out a business model for the film that relied on the sales of toys, a decidedly Disney strategy, to help ensure profitability. Of course, the film's box office alone would have ensured profitability beyond what Lucas might have expected. Lucas made these comments before *Star Wars* even became a box office hit, much less a cultural touchstone. If Lucas had Disney-like aspirations for the *Star Wars* franchise, then as we have noted, Disney's acquisition of Lucasfilm becomes a logical conclusion, one Lucas may not have anticipated when *Star Wars: Episode IV – A New* was released.

By the time of Disney's acquisition of the franchise, however, the circumstances had shifted radically. The original generation of *Star Wars* fans, who made up the audience for the first trilogy of films, constitutes a fan base that is still highly dedicated and sometimes difficult to satisfy. Lucas seems to have first drawn their ire when he included a specifically kid-friendly character – Jar Jar Binks in the first film of the prequel trilogy, *Star Wars: Episode I – The Phantom Menace* (1999). What was seen by some fans as a transparent and disappointing ploy to sell toys and get kids to the theater was seen by other critics as more socially problematic, with Jar Jar Binks being interpreted as a character with racist overtones (Kane, 1999). Subsequently, the character's appearances were minimized in future installments.

Consequently, Jar Jar Binks, and the controversy surrounding him, identifies a point at which Lucas had begun to lose the support of *Star Wars* fans. While fans continued to buy tickets and attend the subsequent films in the prequel trilogy, their complaints escalated, as did their anger toward Lucas. Granted, some of this anger was due to what Lucas was doing with the Indiana Jones franchise, but the dissatisfaction grew to such a level that it attracted the attention of others in the media.

Two examples of critique aimed at *Star Wars* in the immediate years leading up to the Disney merger are worth considering here – the 2010 documentary film *The People vs. George Lucas* and the critiques of George Lucas and *Star Wars* offered by the TV show *South Park* (1997-Present). Alexandre O. Philippe directed *The People vs. George Lucas*, and he has directed other documentaries about popular films such as *Alien* (1979) and *Psycho* (1960). *South Park* is the brainchild of satirists Trey Parker and Matt Stone, who recognize no sacred cows and often employ humor to engage current events and create controversy. As such, their fourth-grade characters stand-in for the children who sat in awe and wonder at the unfolding Lucas universe in the 1970s and 1980s and voice the complaints often raised by disappointed fans.

The People vs. George Lucas is as much about *Star Wars* fandom as it is George Lucas. But there is a through-line that suggests George Lucas has been less than faithful to his fans, often for reasons related to his own business interests or personal peccadilloes and preferences. For example, the film spends some time lamenting Lucas' refusal to release original versions of the *Star Wars* films in digital formats (the original versions are also currently unavailable on Disney+). This is a source of fan frustration in *The People vs. George Lucas*, as Lucas would continue to exercise control over the *Star Wars* franchise and his other properties. The documentary teases out a tension between Lucas' legal and economic right to control the franchise (he created it and, at least at the time *The People vs. George Lucas was* made, owned it), and any sense of ownership the fans might have toward the franchise given their personal attachments, their financial commitment through their consumption, and their advocacy of its virtues to future generations. In *The People vs. George Lucas*, *Star Wars*' power as a cultural phenomenon is due to an investment by the fans. Yet, their investment is discounted and dismissed in the name of Lucas' control and his sense of ownership.

Similar themes are mined in *South Park*. Their critique of George Lucas centers more around a skewering of the Indiana Jones franchise, but the plot of one of the episodes lampooning Lucas, a 2002 episode titled "Free Hat," kicks into gear when the show's four main characters are put off by a digitally remastered version of *The Empire Strikes Back*. Of course, there are some jabs at PC culture ("Wookies" are referred to as "hair challenged" in the fictional remastered cut of the film within the *South Park* episode, for example). But the plot mostly centers on the boys' unsuccessful attempts to stop Lucas (and Steven Spielberg) from remastering *Raiders of the Lost Ark* (1981). They cannot do so, and death and carnage that is a parody of

Raiders of the Lost Ark ensues. In the episode, the boys seem to almost get through to Lucas before a domineering Spielberg reins him in. Lucas tells the boys at one point that he can do what he wants with his movies because "they're mine," foreshadowing a theme in Philippe's film.

South Park has also parodied Disney on several occasions. These episodes usually end up with Mickey Mouse himself showing up and engaging in some awful, over-the-top abuse of power. His exploits on *South Park* have included: blackmailing the Jonas Brothers into sexualizing themselves for young girls, fixing the 2012 presidential election, perpetuating an execution-style killing of Winnie the Pooh, entering into a conspiracy with the Chinese government to frame Hong Kong protesters, and helping cause the COVID-19 outbreak. In *South Park*, we see an articulation of how both the symbol of Disney and the creator of *Star Wars* had come to be viewed with some severe trepidation by the time of the companies' merger. In other words, if fans were concerned about the control that Lucas exercised over *Star Wars*, then the acquisition by Disney of Lucasfilm's offered very cold comfort indeed.

When it comes to Disney's stewardship of the *Star Wars* franchise, the reaction among fans has been decidedly mixed. While some of the films Disney has produced have enjoyed praise from fans and critics alike – *Star Wars: The Force Awakens* (2015) received a 93% Tomatometer score and an 86% audience score on *Rotten Tomatoes*; others have not been as well received. The *Rotten Tomatoes* scores for *Solo* (2018) were 69% and 64%, respectively. Despite this record, the *Star Wars* franchise was a prime property for the launch of Disney+ because the studio hoped it would attract people to the service. To do that, however, it would not be enough to place *Star Wars* on the service, they had to participate in some fan service.

In this chapter, we analyze *The Mandalorian*, which premiered with the launch of Disney+, and we do so from the perspective of fan service. Our analysis differs from that offered in the other chapters in two important ways. Although we believe *The Mandalorian* reflects the Disney style (and we intend to use it as a critical prompt here), we see another strategy at play designed to appease *Star Wars* fans. Therefore, our analysis will also engage elements in the series that evoke fan recognition and references the specialized knowledge that forms within fan cultures (Ott & Walter, 2000). To that end, we also will include an analysis of *Disney Gallery: The Mandalorian*, a paratextual series that was released after the launch of Disney+ (on May 4, 2020). We depart from our previous practice of only considering Disney+ originals that launched with the service for two reasons. First, the series is designed to promote *The Mandalorian* series and explicate its production, so its significance (and existence) depends entirely on the Disney+ original. Second, the series extends the practices of fan service and indirectly and strategically addresses the fan dissatisfaction with George Lucas. We begin with a more detailed history of the relationship connected to the *Star Wars* franchise with the Disney brand. We then move to our analysis of *The Mandalorian* and then turn our attention to the *Disney Gallery: The Mandalorian.*

The Jedi and the Mouse

Star Wars was (and is) well-known as a throwback to film serials of the 1930s and 1940s (Robey, 2015), a kind of homage to retro influences on Lucas' part that, in turn, influenced a lot of contemporary filmmakers who have invoked *Star Wars* in their work. With its fantasy set pieces, clear morality, non-human characters, and adventurous escapades, the film certainly has a Disney ethos. While a complete discussion of how *Star Wars*' narrative and themes line up with Wasko's articulation of Classic Disney tropes (Wasko, 2001) is outside the scope of this chapter, that style has a lot in common with *Star Wars*. The *Star Wars* films clearly articulate such values as individualism, magic, romance, innocence, etc. Further, the series' "space western" categorization hints at the impact of Western-themed fare for which Disney was also known in the early days of television (Andreychuk, 2005). Disney was one of several studios to which Lucas unsuccessfully shopped the original film. As we have noted, Lucas considered it appropriate for the studio. We can only conjecture that the rejection that Lucas received from Disney might have inspired his charge of abdication. In any event, *Star Wars* was in important ways a Disney film some three decades before a lucrative business deal made it legally and formally so. Disney's reticence to get into the *Star Wars* business was shared by other studios who also passed on the project. This rejection was understandable given the state of the film industry in the mid- to late 1970s. This was the era of big, important contemporary dramas in the vein of *Godfather* (1972), *Raging Bull* (1980), *Chinatown* (1974), and even *Coming Home* (1978); films that said something about the US, its turbulent political and social context, and its weary citizens. *Star Wars* was a groundbreaking film, an unexpected success, and a missed opportunity for all the studios that passed on the project, but it was especially so for Disney.

Indeed, one could argue that the popularity of *Star Wars* spurred Disney to begin chasing after its own signature sci-fi, action/adventure titles with *The Black Hole*, *Tron*, and *Dragonslayer* (1981) all sprouting out of the studio. Of course, no Disney offering in the years immediately following *Star Wars* had the financial or cultural impact of Lucas' brainchild. However, as Disney was attempting to build its own *Star Wars*, 20th Century Fox was attempting to capitalize on the success of the film in a very Disney-like manner.

The rather infamous *Star Wars Holiday Special* aired on the CBS network on November 17, 1978. The special was primarily product-driven by 20th Century Fox, and George Lucas had little involvement. Consequently, his lack of affinity for the franchise's holiday special stretches back decades and is well-documented (Higgins, 2019). The primary plot of the special involves Han Solo and Chewbacca making their way to Chewbacca's home planet for the celebration of a holiday called "Life Day." Chewbacca's family eagerly awaits his return, enlisting Luke Skywalker's aid to ascertain his whereabouts when the trip takes longer than expected; Chewie and Han are delayed because of their involvement in interstellar, Imperial trouble. This plot provides a rather loose framing device for the variety of entertainment the special includes. Several original cast members appeared, including Mark Hamill, Harrison Ford, and Carrie Fisher (who gets to sing). Other musical performances were provided by Diahann Carroll and Jefferson Starship, who show up to perform numbers that are derived from the film's plot. Inexplicably, except that they all enjoyed popularity on television and in film at the time, the cast also included Harvey Korman, Bea Arthur, and Art Carney.

Consequently, *Star Wars Holiday Special* seemed to be quite a departure from the original film. It was generally panned at the time (Acuna, 2015). However, it has enjoyed some admittedly ironic enjoyment from *Star Wars* fans over the years. Ultimately, however, 20th Century Fox did a poor job with this variety special. It begs the question: how would the show have been handled if it were produced by a different studio, Disney, for example?

In ways, the special seems to be firmly within Disney's wheelhouse. As we noted in a previous chapter, Disney certainly had experience producing successful television variety shows. In the tradition of *The Wonderful World of Disney*, *Star Wars Holiday Special* involved a repurposing of 20th Century Fox's intellectual property for a television film in a way that straddles the line between content, branding, and mixing genres. For example, the way the pop music numbers are integrated into the plot reflects a typical content strategy related to music in Disney films that can be traced back to *Snow White* (1937) and that persists even today. "A Whole New World" (1992) from *Aladdin* (1992) was performed by popular R & B artists Regina Belle and Peabo Bryson. "You'll be in my Heart" (1999) from *Tarzan* (1999) was performed by Phil Collins, arguably one the most popular musician, in terms of chart success, of the 1980s and 1990s. Elton John capped off a half-decade-long comeback and cemented a new generation of fans with "Circle of Life" (1994) and "Can You Feel the Love Tonight" (1994) from *The Lion King* (1994). Even in more contemporary times, "Let it Go" (2013) from *Frozen* (2013) traded on Idina Menzel's growing popularity. The songs from various Disney films have stood on their own as culturally relevant musical numbers for decades. While 20th Century Fox probably hoped for similar success with the music in the holiday special, they fell far short of Disney's record.

Star Wars Holiday Special also introduces the concept of family into the franchise. However, as of the special's airing, only the original *Star Wars* film had been released. The *Star Wars* saga is the story of the Skywalker family, with a focus on father and son relationships, with that narrative through-line continuing to the Disney-era trilogy focusing on Han Solo's tragic relationship with his son, Kylo Ren (one that serves as the dark shadow of the father and son relationship that drives the original trilogy). Yet Vader was not revealed to be Luke Skywalker's father until the second film in the series, 1980s *The Empire Strikes Back*, and Luke and Leia were not revealed to be siblings until 1983s *The Return of the Jedi*. In addition, Luke's adventure is motivated by the loss of the family he knew in the first film. As such, family, a decidedly Disney motif and target audience, was not a part of the *Star Wars* mythology before the release of the holiday special that focused heavily on both Chewbacca's odyssey to get to his family and on what life was like for a family of Wookies. These narrative beats hearken back to (and foreshadow) any number of Disney classics about the challenges and dynamics families (that seem simultaneously human and non-human) face. The film even delves some into the nature of Wookie culture, just as many Disney films outline cultures of other lands, realities, and societies. Indeed, *Star Wars Holiday Special* can be read as purely a show about a family with a lost member looking for a way back – it can be seen as, say, a narrative bridge between something like *Bambi* (1942) and *The Lion King*.

The holiday special also echoes Disney storytelling in that it mixes live-action and animation. The incorporation of live-action and animation can be traced back to the beginning of Walt's career when he produced the *Alice Comedies* in 1923 (Thomas, 1994). This not only places it structurally in line with Disney television and film presentation and style, but it marks *Star Wars'* entry into animation, Disney's forte. The holiday special also marked the first appearance of Boba Fett (Kuchera, 2015), a character whose legacy would be critical to the Disney/*Star Wars* union several decades later. Boba Fett has also proven to be a very popular character in *Star Wars* mythology (Kring-Schreifels, 2019). This makes it particularly ironic that the character emerged from the holiday special, in animated form no less. The character is a bounty hunter who is a member of a warrior class known as Mandalorians in *Star Wars* mythology. Indeed, Boba Fett is central enough to the *Star Wars* franchise that Disney+ has made *Star Wars Holiday Special* segment that features him available for streaming (Vary, 2021) despite the rest of the show's persona non grata status.

In other words, the narrative for the Disney+ original series *The Mandalorian* can be traced back to this special. Therefore, while this special was not a Disney production, it would be integral to Disney's production of *The Mandalorian*. Paradoxically, although Lucas embraced Disney as an influence for *Star Wars* while disavowing the holiday special, this special was important as a textual bridge to Disney in the ways we have identified.

This relationship between Disney and *Star Wars* became more formal in the 1980s with the advent of *Star Wars* attractions at Disney theme parks (Ratcliffe, 2014). "Star Tours" was the first such attraction. It opened in the Tomorrowland section of Disneyland in 1987, linking the park to a famous sci-fi brand when Tomorrowland was becoming a bit dated. This was a significant development because it was the first major attraction in the park that was not based on Disney's intellectual property. Other *Star Wars* attractions would follow, opening at Tokyo Disneyland, Disney World, and Paris Disneyland. The *Star Wars* theme park attractions further paved the way for a Disney/Lucas union in some more tangible ways. For example, these attractions placed *Star Wars* characters, themes, and merchandise in the same physical space as Disney products and narratives. Further, it allowed Disney fans to immerse themselves in the physical space and narratives of *Star Wars*, and it allowed *Star Wars* fans to do the same with Disney spaces and narratives. The theme parks provided a way to keep the union between the two alive and to further promote cross-pollination between the two different fan bases.

By the turn of the millennium, though, Disney's fortunes were improving, primarily aided by their collaborations with Pixar, which, as we noted in a previous chapter, was formerly a Lucasfilm property (Govindarajan, 2016). Lucasfilm, noticing the popularity of the Pixar/Disney collaborations, decided to launch Lucasfilm Animation in 2003. The studio expanded the Star Wars universe, focusing on CGI animation (Pixar's strength). More specifically, this move produced *The Clone Wars* (2008) animated series, which brought David Filoni into Lucasfilm, who later becomes a significant contributor to *The Mandalorian.* As Disney would move away from cell animation, producing CGI offerings under both the Disney and Pixar label, the launch of Lucasfilm Animation was yet another way that the studios began to overlap. Yet, when the merger finally took place, Disney had acquired a franchise that had been significantly diminished by its creator (Lucas), and that would present a problem that would need to be addressed. Or, more to the point, Disney inherited a fan base that would need to be addressed very carefully.

Fan Service, *Star Wars*, and Disney

The concept of fan service in media studies is, at once, both a reasonably new concept and one steeped in some important pre-existing scholarly traditions. Fan service tends to describe efforts made to specifically please or cater to fans' interests of a particular show, film, or other media product (Epstein, 2018). While it is easy to see how the concept is especially relevant today with so much media and pop culture relying on adaptations, remakes, reboots, existing intellectual property, leveraging existing brands, etc., the concept has its roots in an array of mid-20th-century academic and critical trends. Reception studies and reader-response criticism formed the basis of understanding texts from the perspective of audiences. Hall (1973) introduced such concepts as encoding, decoding, oppositional readings, and negotiation of meaning to give some form to the ways audiences might resist intended meanings of texts and/or work with them to subvert preferred readings. Indeed, when today's fans of *Star Wars* take to Twitter to complain about or to lament deviations from the source material, one can see digital era variations on Hall's ideas at work.

Radaway's (1984) study of romance fiction influences contemporary fan studies in a couple of important ways. Radaway's work attempted to redeem a supposedly marginalized form of popular culture whose audience was often disparaged. Radaway noted that reading a text is a social event, thereby recognizing how fan cultures emerge through collective consumption. Following Radaway, a host of other audience-centric media criticism of the 1980s and 1990s also contributed to a critical context that sought to understand audiences, fans, and fandom. For example, Fiske (1987) expanded the study of audiences and their reception of texts into various distinct contours of popular culture.

In the new millennium's increasingly digital culture, the relationship between fans and media corporations has seen significant shifts, allowing fans a variety of public platforms. Early in the digital age, some media corporations pushed back against various fan critiques or copyright violations. Jenkins (2006) outlined one prominent example of this with his discussion of how Warner Bros. cracked down hard on *Harry Potter* (2001) fan fiction. The recent Warner/HBO Max reversal on the *Justice League* Snyder cut (2021) illustrates the role fan feedback played in that it provides a notable example of how much the playing field has leveled in the past couple of decades.

Fan service recognizes the agency of audience reception and attempts to address that agency in ways that enhance the fan experience, thereby increasing intellectual property value. For example, Carrington (2019) highlights how *Black Panther* specifically articulates and invokes various narratives, styles, and historical experiences central to African American culture (primarily grounded in blaxploitation films of the 1960s and 1970s) as a specific type of fan service to that audience and community. Fan service is also important to television production and promotion. Scolari (2013) outlines how the creators of *Lost* (2004) crafted an array of supplemental, paratextual content – much of it blurring the lines between fiction and reality – to deploy on the internet or at fan conventions to keep the audience engaged and to fill in narrative gaps in the show. Prior investment in the show's complicated mythology motivated existing fans to seek out and consume these paratexts, and this brings us to the relationship between paratexts and fan service.

Many contemporary fan service strategies borrow from ideas related to intertextuality (Kristeva, 1980), which become manifest in paratextual strategies. Paratexts were originally theorized to explain how literary texts derive meaning from book covers, promotional campaigns, interviews, and book reviews (Genette, 1997). Brookey and Gray (2017) have noted that paratexts have become increasingly common in contemporary media practices and have been used for fan service. Indeed, Beaty (2016) has demonstrated how paratextual practices of meta storytelling, references to other pop culture, Easter eggs, post-credit sequences, callbacks, interlinked stories, and insider narratives have all emerged as prominent paratextual fan service strategies.

Reaching the *Star Wars* fan base became an immediate concern because complaints about Disney's ownership of Lucasfilm began almost as soon as the merger was announced (Schwartzel & Watson, 2019). While the new *Star Wars* films produced under the Disney banner have elicited mixed reactions from *Star Wars* fans, this discontent with the franchise is not unique to or caused by Disney's acquisition. As we have noted, there is general fan skepticism that dates back to the prequel trilogy. There is also the problem of trying to appeal to different generations – the older *Star Wars* fans who grew up with the original series and their children who have different expectations and tastes. Arguably, this desire to reach across different generational fan bases has resulted in some somewhat repetitive storytelling. Indeed, the Disney-era trilogy is another story of another Skywalker (albeit on the mother's side) tempted by the dark side, really the third time that story has been told. *Solo*, the Han Solo prequel film, can be seen as an excuse to replace an aging Harrison Ford with Alden Ehrenreich as a young Han Solo. To that end, the film follows the character through an origin story that shows him meeting Chewbacca and Lando Calrissian (familiar and important supporting characters for Han Solo) along the way. Darth Maul even shows up as a kind of refugee from the prequel trilogy. Although this film provided more detail to this character's backstory, it did not move the franchise's narrative forward in a compelling way. The box office and critical reception showed a lack of enthusiasm for the material. *Rogue One* (2016), by way of contrast, seems to stand as an original entry in the franchise in terms of story and style, and it made over 2.5 times the box office of *Solo* (Katz, 2020).

If Star Wars purists were worried Disney would make striking changes to the franchise – they need not have fretted. Indeed, *The Mandalorian* illustrates Disney's desire to appease fans by tapping into the various elements of the *Star Wars* franchise and universe and making sure those elements are readily recognized. Yet the series also moves the franchise into new territory and introduces new characters. However, these new elements are designed to appeal to fans. In the analysis that follows, we begin by identifying practices of fan service in the series, then show how that fan service is augmented by the paratextual strategies of *Disney Gallery: The Mandalorian* series. Specifically, we see this paratextual series appealing to the specialized knowledge that is often at the heart of fan cultures while also addressing the context of the fan revolt against George Lucas (Ott & Walter, 2000).

Enter The Mandalorian

Set several years after the events of *Return of the Jedi, The Mandalorian* serves as a sequel to the original *Star Wars* trilogy and as a prequel to the Disney-era new trilogy. The series centers on a Mandalorian bounty hunter ultimately revealed to be named Din Djarin, hired by leftover Imperial loyalists, headed by a mysterious figure known as The Client, to capture an equally mysterious target. While scant information is given about the target, Djarin is told that the target is 50 years old. So, he is surprised to find an infant-sized creature when he locates the bounty. The target seems to be of the same species as Yoda, the legendary Jedi master in the *Star Wars* films. Djarin is unaware that Yoda's species age more slowly; indeed, he is unaware of the species in general or most Galactic/Rebel Alliance conflicts. After a shootout with a droid intent on killing the target, Djarin decides to protect the child rather than turn it over to The Client. The remainder of the series' first season follows the exploits of Djarin and the Yoda-like creature, known as The Child (and popularly referred to as Baby Yoda by many fans) as they traverse the galaxy trying to elude various entities who seek to capture The Child or claim a bounty that has been placed on Djarin for his refusal to surrender The Child.[1] Ultimately The Client is revealed to be working with a former Imperial leader, Moff Gideon, who wants to exploit The Child's connection to The Force (the mysterious energy that defines Jedis). Along the way, Djarin makes alliances with several characters – some temporary and some more permanent – including former Rebel fighter Cara Dune, bounty hunter bureaucrat Greef Karga, and even a droid that was tasked with killing The Child.

Some episodes are standalone. Some propel the show's mythology surrounding the Mandalorian race and The Child, with Djarin learning more about Mandalorian legacies, Jedis, Imperial/Republic tensions, and his personal history as a childhood survivor of the Clone Wars. Djarin frequently finds himself in odd parts of the galaxy, often having to combat some oppressive or sinister threat to the community he is visiting. As the first season of *The Mandalorian* draws to a close, The Child is saved from a kidnapping plot by Gideon. Djarin learns there are still some Jedi left in the galaxy. A Mandalorian tribal leader known as The Armorer cements the father/son bond between The Mandalorian and The Child. Djarin then sets out to find a Jedi who can adequately train The Child. In a subsequent season, that Jedi is revealed to be none other than Luke Skywalker. And, indeed, The Child's tutelage at the hands of Luke Skywalker is itself a part of the subsequent *Boba Fett* spinoff series.

It is worth noting that the animated series *The Clone Wars* establishes a broader backstory for the Mandalorians, a fictional class of warriors within the *Star Wars* universe. As we noted earlier, the first Mandalorian in *Star Wars* mythology, Boba Fett, was introduced in animated form in the holiday special. It is also worth noting that the show introduced a live-action version of a character from *The Clone Wars* animated series, Ahsoka Tano (Thorne, 2020), further cementing its reliance on content grounded in animation. Therefore, the intertextual reference of the series to previous properties and narrative elements of the *Star Wars* universe appeals to fans' particular knowledge and evokes Disney's signature genre.

The series may be called *The Mandalorian*, but the show's star is almost certainly the toddler Din Djarin saves and takes under his wing. The Child is an infant member of Yoda's species with budding, sometimes uncontrollable, sometimes misused versions of all of Yoda's powers – thus the moniker "Baby Yoda." With The Child/Baby Yoda character, Disney cleverly borrows the essence of a *Star Wars* character (Yoda) but packages it in a way that recalls not only Mickey Mouse but any number of cute, anthropomorphic non-human characters designed to service the storytelling and marketing interests of children, families, and Disney fans. The connection to established Disney characters is further emphasized by using animals for some of Baby Yoda's vocal sounds (Russell, 2020). So, The Child/Baby Yoda stands as an example of Disney doing what it does best – creating a loveable, child-friendly character.

Of course, to say Disney knows how to deploy such a character might lead one to assume that The Child/Baby Yoda entered pop culture consciousness via a marketing blitz replete with toys, collectibles, and clothing before the series' release. Although the series was released close to Thanksgiving, Disney did not release any merchandise for this new character before the Disney+, launch, a surprising move considering Disney's marketing prowess. As Nick Venable noted in *Cinemablend* (2019), the withholding of merchandise was strategic, and Jon Favreau has remarked that they wanted to save the reveal of the character for the show.

The Child the name given to the character in shooting scripts came to be known popularly as "Baby Yoda" via social media posts and memes. Disney introduced the character with little to no fanfare and never formally named the character during the show's first season. This allowed the fanbase to feel ownership of the character and connect with him in an interactive fashion. The first Baby Yoda merchandise was also generally fan-made, often available via websites like Etsy. Disney at least waited until their merchandise was ready before turning their lawyers loose on unlicensed merchandise (Gartenberg, 2020). For weeks, Baby Yoda dominated trending lists on Twitter, commentary on social networks, reviews of *The Mandalorian*, and commentary from business analysts (Vasquez, 2019). Even *South Park* seemed to like Baby Yoda. With The Child/Baby Yoda, Disney has taken a decidedly contemporary strategy via fan-generated, viral content through memes and fan merchandise. They simply put the character out there and let his popularity grow organically, a simultaneous union of fan service and marketing. It is a strategy that worked. Once the series premiered, the merchandise followed; in fact, a search on Amazon using "Baby Yoda" at around that time rendered seven pages of different products.[2] Clearly, the character has an established footprint in the ancillary market. This market has proven significant to both Lucasfilm and Disney.

During this early period of the character's evolution, merchandise on the Shop Disney website referred to him like this: *The Child, affectionately known as Baby Yoda* (Shop Disney, n.d.). In the past, Disney might have had their lawyers scrub all references to the Baby Yoda nickname from the internet. However, in a digital culture, it makes good business sense to let such an overwhelmingly accepted fan choice remain, if only informally. It is particularly important that Disney refashioned its sometimes overly traditional methods to adhere to digital culture norms in the context of a streaming service. Baby Yoda serves as an example of successfully merging the *Star Wars* style and the Disney style and deploying it in a contemporary, fan-driven, digital context.

Baby Yoda is at once a Disney character and a *Star Wars* character – he has many of the characteristics of traditional Disney "cuteness," while also having many characteristics of a specific beloved *Star Wars* character (Yoda). He satisfies the norms, expectations, and values of both Disney and *Star Wars* fans. Further, he is placed within a storyline that is familiar to both *Star Wars* and Disney fans – hanging out with a Mandalorian and getting into space hijinks for the *Star Wars* fans; and moving tentatively through life as a special being guided toward destiny by a mythic parental figure, a la Bambi, Simba, or Pinocchio, for the Disney fans. The character's story arc serves the expectations of both groups of fans. Of course, this structure allows for invoking various strategies related to intertextuality and irony associated with many fan service strategies. Indeed, the character's double-barreled Disney/*Star Wars* ethos has arguably been borrowed from heavily to craft the particular contours of the Young Princess Leia character in the subsequent *Obi-Wan Kenobi* series (Donaldson, 2022).

In another important act of fan service, *The Mandalorian* marks a step toward correcting some of the storytelling problems associated with Disney-era *Star Wars* content. As the previous section discussed, there seemed to be a lack of originality or reinvention in some of those films. However, *The Mandalorian* uses those familiar beats as new points of connection for the franchise narrative. The show's title character arguably follows in the footsteps of Boba Fett, Han Solo, Obi-Wan Kenobi, and even Yoda, ironically. The relationship between the title character and The Child/Baby Yoda is equal parts Luke and Yoda, Obi-Wan and Anakin, and Han Solo and Chewbacca. The story is set after the events of the original *Star Wars* films but before the events of the Disney-era films. Several main characters are survivors of the various intergalactic conflicts that seem to constantly plague that galaxy. Din Djarin, the main character's birth name, is a survivor of the Clone Wars, depicted in the prequel trilogy and the subsequent animated series. One of his sidekicks, Cara Dune, is a former member of the rebel alliance with some Empire-induced baggage. The series is set in a world that has been rocked by the intergalactic strife of the persistent struggle between the Empire and the Rebels. However, the space politics take a back seat and allow those impacted by them to take center stage, thereby refiguring the old conflicts into new dramatic tension, with new characters, different stakes, and jeopardy.

Indeed, some characters, the title character included, seem ignorant of some fundamental aspects of *Star Wars* mythology. For example, when The Child/Baby Yoda's species is explained to Din Djarin, Jedis are treated as something foreign and mystical, something akin to how supernatural characters in a Bible story might be explained to someone. The title character broadly understands that what he learns means The Child/Baby Yoda comes from an enemy species. However, he has no context for what all that might tangibly mean. By setting the series in a world that was more indirectly impacted by Luke, Obi-Wan, and Anakin/Vader's endless conflicts, and by focusing on characters who are similar to, but also distinctly detached from, traditional *Star Wars* characters, the show crafts a narrative that attempts to reinvigorate the franchise. In other words, the show gives the fans the common elements of the *Star Wars* universe but takes the narrative of the franchise in new directions. This last statement seems to be the overarching thesis of the paratextual *The Disney Gallery: The Mandalorian.*

The Disney Gallery: The Mandalorian

This eight-episode series revolves around various participants in, and aspects of, the production of *The Mandalorian*, and the episodes take us behind the scenes of the making of the series. In ways, these episodes are extended versions of the electronic press kits that are prepared to market new media content, and they serve a similar promotional paratextual function. Each episode is anchored by Jon Favreau, credited as the Executive Producer and Creator of *The Mandalorian*. Often serving as his co-anchor is Dave Filoni, also an Executive Producer, who shares directing and writing credit on some of the episodes. In between footage shot on set during production, Favreau leads group discussions among various actors and crew members, reminiscent of Favreau's IFC series *Dinner for Five* (2001). We should note that both Favreau and Filoni also share production credit on this paratextual series. Although the show is promotional in its purpose, the series has the depth and production values that have marked the Disney brand of promotion (*The Wonderful World of Disney* is a case in point). Each episode of the series is devoted to a topic titled accordingly: "Directing," "Technology," "Process." Included are episodes entitled "Legacy" and "Connections," and in these episodes, the fan service is most pronounced; although, it is present in other episodes as well.

Gestures toward fan service begin with the first episode, devoted to the directors of the series (including Byrce Dallas Howard, Rick Famuyiwa, Deborah Chow, and Taika Waititi). The episode begins with Filoni pointing to footage and commenting, "Did you see, you can see the laser in his helmet? Amazing what we get excited about around here, 'Look, a laser!'" The video then cuts to footage of two spaceships from the series engaged in a laser battle. In this way, the series begins by addressing the viewer as a fan, one who can perhaps identify with Filoni's excitement, as his own fan identity is clearly on display. This episode reveals how all the directors involved in the first season approached the series informed by their own fan identities. Favreau begins the roundtable discussion with the directors by stating, "The one thing that unifies us is that we all love *Star Wars*."

Filoni, who had previously worked on *The Clone Wars*, relates how he was interviewed and hired by Lucas for the animated series. He remarks that after the interview, even though he thought he did not get the job, "all I could think is that when I'm in line for *Revenge of the Sith* (2005), I can outclass any nerd there because I've been in a room with George Lucas." He then discloses all the details about the *Star Wars* universe that Lucas discussed during the interview, and Filoni claims the conversation "was incredible validation for all the arguments that I had with friends." In other words, Filoni speaks to his own fan experience as one who stands in line with other fans for the films and argues with his friends about the details of the Star Wars Universe. He also got the job on *The Clone Wars*.

The other directors also offer different but similar fan bona fides. Deborah Chow mentions how she has always been a fan of the sci-fi and action/adventure genres. Famuyiwa notes that "Star Wars was a big part of my life, and a big part of who I am creatively. . .*Star Wars* was the first film I saw in a theater." He goes on to suggest that this experience shaped his perspective on film and storytelling. On the other hand, Howard relates a story of going on a business trip to Japan with her father (Ron Howard) when she was young. During this trip, her father took her to dinner with Lucas and the director Akira Kurosawa. Although she admits falling asleep during the dinner, she claims the experience has stayed with her.

In other words, Howard, like Filoni, has her own experience with Lucas, and these comments about Lucas reveal a rhetorical strategy of this paratext. Despite the fan revolt we mentioned earlier, in this *Disney Gallery*, Lucas is very much embraced and arguably exalted. For example, the "Legacy" episode begins with Favreau on set. He mentions that "we are trying to draw from all over from *Star Wars*. It's helpful for authenticity." As we are shown various actors and crew members interacting, he comments, "I've always been a fan since I was little, and now I'm surrounded by other fans, too." Here Favreau identifies with *Star Wars* fans and extends that point of identification to the cast and crew; he also suggests that he and the cast and crew are also mindful and respectful of the *Star Wars* legacy. Soon we discover that respect also extends to George Lucas.

For this episode, Favreau and Filoni are joined by John Knoll, an ILM Visual Effects Supervisor, who has known and/or worked with George Lucas for several years. Knoll mentions that he was inspired to enter the industry because of *Star Wars*, and he took a job at ILM in the hopes that he would get to work on a future *Star Wars* film. His first was *Episode I: Phantom Menace*. He worked on the other two trilogy films and *Rogue One: A Star Wars Story* and *The Mandalorian*. The scene cuts to a solo interview with Filoni in which he remarks that some people do not fully appreciate the creative vision that Lucas has brought to *Star Wars*:

> I like to think that I do, but I worked with him, so I've seen him create it. I've seen the person who comes up with the lines of dialogue and understands Anakin Skywalker and Luke Skywalker in a very deep level because those characters are a part of him.

Here Filoni positions Lucas as the primary creative force behind the franchise. Later he notes that although he felt privileged to contribute to the *Star Wars* story, he always depended on Lucas for input and direction because "It's his story . . . he created the universe."

Although this episode does much to credit Lucas with the *Star Wars* legacy, it also suggests that the production of *The Mandalorian* is a continuation of that legacy, even though Lucas is not directly involved in the production. For example, Howard avers that Lucas was always interested in collaboration and that "he really understood that the characters are meant to expand in ways that George might not even predict. . .He's always wanted to push the story in directions that include other storytellers." Famuyiwa recalls his youthful obsession with *Star Wars* in which he saw opportunities for his own storytelling, actualized in play with his friends and his action figures. In other words, Famuyiwa sees his participation in the production of *The Mandalorian* as extending from his youthful imagination, which was, in turn, inspired by Lucas.

During these discussions of Lucas, we are shown various behind-the-scenes footage, some of it featuring Lucas. He is often shown holding a cup of coffee, observing, and occasionally chatting with the crew and the cast. Therefore, this episode of the series literally and figuratively brings Lucas into the room. However, it does not appear that they let him touch anything.[3] As the title of the episode suggests, the Lucas legacy informs *The Mandalorian*. However, as with many legacies, it has been passed on to the creators of this new series, who, as Howard attests, are different storytellers pushing the story in different directions. In other words, where *The Mandalorian* is concerned, Lucas is an influence, but he is no longer the storyteller.

Although these references to Lucas may appear to be contrary to the task of fan service, their importance will become clear later. Setting these preferences aside, for now, we turn our attention to more apparent gestures to fan service present in the paratextual series. For example, an episode entitled "Connections" begins with Favreau observing how elements that appear in *The Mandalorian* have been culled from the *Star Wars* video games and

The Clone Wars. He then leads a discussion about what he considers one of the "deep cuts," the appearance of an ice cream maker. The ice cream maker first appears in *The Empire Strikes Back*, carried by an extra who runs through a scene. As Favreau explains, the fans have embraced this character (Willrow Hood), and some show up at conventions and events dressed as Hood carrying the ice maker. In *The Mandalorian*, the same object now is invested with greater narrative purpose, and as Favreau notes, "like in Pulp Fiction, when you open the briefcase." In this case, the ice cream maker holds the bounty for "the Asset" (Baby Yoda).

Later in the episode, Favreau explains how the fans were bought into the production of *The Mandalorian*. The 501st Legion is a cosplay organization, the members of which construct and dress up in their Stormtrooper armor, attend various events, and are actively involved in charity work. Lucasfilm has called on the 501st to appear at certain promotional events, but they had never been asked to appear on screen until *The Mandalorian*. Several members of the 501st are interviewed for the episode. They remark that they had no idea they would appear in the series until they were brought on set. As Favreau notes, the members of the 501st enhanced their scenes by adding to the number of background actors, and they fit into the scenes seamlessly because they already knew how to move and act like Stormtroopers. Their inclusion in the series was a realization of a dream often held by those who cosplay: to appear in the narrative they are attempting to reproduce with their costumes. One of the 501st remarks that "this is a dream," and we would suggest that making fans' dreams come true is a very strong form of fan service.

Yet, the "connections" do not end there. Later in this episode, it is revealed how some of the directors (Filoni, Chow, and Famuyiwa) appear in the series as X-wing fighters, which were shot at Favreau's insistence. These very brief scenes, in which Filoni, Chow, and Famuyiwa are each given one line, were shot on a practical X-wing prop that then was moved to the Orlando park and installed as part of the Galaxy's Edge attraction. While Filoni admits to some reluctance about the scene, Favreau argues that "fans are going to love it." We agree, and here is why: this paratext aligns these directors with the 501st, as fans who get to appear in the narrative of *Star Wars*. In this way, a connection is made between the fans, the material, and the creators of that material. A connection heightened for those who visit the X-wing in Orlando, all for the park admission price, and can encounter the actual prop occupied by these directors.

As for George Lucas, the references now begin to make more sense. The artists behind the production of *The Mandalorian* are positioned as fans, with knowledge and respect for the material. In turn, their respect for Lucas harkens back to a time when fans shared that respect. Where *The Mandalorian* is concerned, however, the fans have taken over from Lucas in continuing the *Star Wars* mythos, and this paratext assures us that the legacy is in good hands. At the end of the "Legacy" episode, Filoni explains why *Star Wars* "works and why we care." As he explains, while the special effects and gadgetry are significant, *Star Wars* presents us with a story to which we can "soulfully react . . . we don't just want an action movie, we want to be uplifted." He notes the narrative arch of the franchise instills in us a sense of hope, "that we fundamentally want to be good people, that we can all be driven to do terrible things, but that we can persevere through selfless actions." He concludes that this sense of hope can be attributed to Lucas: "something he has reiterated most times I've seen him . . . after we have been making things without him, 'Remember to make these stories hopeful. Remember to give that to kids, because they really need it.'" In this way, *The Disney Gallery* redeems Lucas to set him to the side and put Favreau, Filoni, and the other series creatives in his place. Fans can rest assured that the *Star Wars* narrative is now being extended by those who understand the legacy but are mindful of the fans' interest because they are fans themselves.

It is also important to note how Filoni's comments posit optimism as the *Star Wars* mythos' central core value, which brings us back to the Classic Disney style. *The Mandalorian* series has some decidedly Disney flourishes to the story. Baby Yoda is the ultimate in neoterized characters, a 50-year-old baby, and although the character is not an animal per se, it is more animal than human (at least where the sound effects are concerned). In contrast to Din Djarin, the character is innocent not only to the threats in his environment but also to the power he uses to contain those threats. As an abandoned character, The Child evokes the innocence and jeopardy of Bambi, while Din Djarin's role as a surrogate father fuels the narrative as he must accept the responsibilities that come with that role. In this way, his role as a protector is more in line with Mufasa or Geppetto than Darth Vader. The villains, while still of *Star Wars* stock, also reflect the formula that produced Disney villains. Their motives align with Amos Slade or Cruella De Vil in terms of idiosyncratic obsession and greed. While Disney-era *Star Wars* films have had mixed results and at times struggled to serve traditional *Star Wars* fan expectations, *The Mandalorian* has introduced both a new *Star Wars*-style hero that blends a classic and revisionist take on the franchise; and, simultaneously, introduced a decidedly Disney character in The Child/Baby Yoda.

Happy Now?

If reviews are any indication, and we believe they are, then *The Mandalorian* can be seen as a project that successfully blends the Disney brand with the Star Wars universe. The first season received a 93% rating on *Rotten Tomatoes* and a 91% audience score. Some reviewers considered the series in relation to the problems of fan service, and even in that regard, consider the series a success. For example, in his review for *The Sydney Morning Herald*, Michael Idato (2019) writes:

> *Star Wars* is a hard nut to crack open. Getting it right means dancing along a perilous algorithm, first created in our childhood, when our judgment was dulled by spectacular space dogfights and the clash of duelling (sic) lightsabers, replicated in the world's backyard using broom and mop handles. It is likely nothing will ever match that. But *The Mandalorian* comes stunningly, unexpectedly, brilliantly close.
>
> (para. 8)

In addition, some critics have also noted how the series successfully revives the franchise and moves away from the overused narrative tropes that have often plagued the films. For example, on *Salon*, Melanie McFarland notes:

> The fact that its repeating themes are being met with lower levels of patience with the release of each new film indicates how hungry we are for a new beginning and a fresh paradigm. And this makes "The Mandalorian" a successful bridge between the old and a tantalizing unknown, expanding our gaze into worlds and people few have bothered to explore in-depth because we were so obsessed with Skywalkers and Organas and Solos and Palpatine's.
>
> (2019, para. 28, 29)

In other words, McFarland recognizes that the franchise has been given over to new storytellers with new stories. The evidence that fans have embraced these new stories was cemented after the second season of *The Mandalorian* when it was announced that the series had bested *The Office* (2005) as the most-watched show on a streaming service (Clark, 2021). Therefore, the series seems to have successfully appeased the dissatisfaction of *Star Wars* fans, and the paratextual series probably helped secure this success by containing the controversy surrounding Lucas.

Yet, while Disney may have appeased fans where the Lucas controversy was concerned, following the successful conclusion of the second season of *The Mandalorian*, they were soon confronting another. Gina Carano, who portrayed Cara Dune in the series, was fired by Lucasfilm and Disney after posts she had made to social media claiming that Donald Trump's loss in the 2020 election had been a product of voter fraud. She also shared posts that disparaged those who wore masks during the pandemic, and members of the transgender community. The firing occurred on February 10, 2021, shortly after Carano compared the treatment of Republicans to the Holocaust. According to *The Hollywood Reporter*, Carano was warned about her social media posting before being fired (Couch, Siegel & Kit, 2021). Consequently, Carano was embraced by conservatives and right-wing media as yet another victim of cancel culture. Days after her firing was announced, she was interviewed by political conservative Ben Shapiro, in which she described her treatment by Disney as "bullying" and attributed this treatment to the company's liberal political motives (Yasharoff, 2021).

When questioned about the controversy, current Disney CEO Bob Chapek denied any corporate political bias and argued that the company is informed by values such as integrity and inclusion (Trepany, 2021). While Chapek may believe this to be true, we should note that his predecessor, Bob Iger, was very vocal in his support of the Biden/Harris ticket and had voiced that support on social media no less (Haring, 2021). However, we would maintain that Carano's firing had as much to do with brand optics as it did with politics. Whether intentional or not, Carano's comments were in support of the same political factions that were responsible for the violent attacks that occurred in Washington on January 6, 2021. The actions of that day were rendered in visual imagery that was decidedly off-brand for Disney. By aligning herself with the perpetrators of that violence, Carano was also going off-brand.

As for the bullying, Carano's comments certainly beg the question: did she know anything about the company that was signing her checks? When it comes to defending their brand, Disney has no compunction about bringing its vast legal resources into battles with small independent businesses, including day centers and bakeries. Perhaps Carano should have watched the episode of *South Park* where the Jonas brothers were beaten into submission by Mickey. In any event, Carano should have known that what is most important to Disney is not politics but the company brand. And if you are going to be employed by Disney for a high-profile project, then you had better also be a good ambassador for that brand. In other words, if you are going to work for Disney, you had better whistle while you do so. For example, in the next chapter, we consider *The World According to Jeff Goldblum*, and in that show, it becomes readily apparent that Goldblum knows how to work and whistle.

Notes

1 In the second season, the character's name was revealed to be Grogu. We refer to the character as either The Child or Baby Yoda throughout because those were the two names associated with the character at the time of the first season's airing.
2 Our own search was conducted on March 2, 2021.
3 At this point we should note that Lucas has been vocal about his dissatisfaction with Disney's *Star Wars* films. Indeed, he's apparently so bothered by them that he has begun speculating about a return to the franchise (McGloin, 2020).

References

Acuna, K. (2015, December 15). I just watched the infamous 'Star Wars Holiday Special' and I finally understand why it only aired once. *Business Insider*. Retrieved from https://www.businessinsider.com/the-star-wars-holiday-special-review-2015-12

Andrews, T. (2019, October 14). Disney spent the day reminding us of the truly bizarre films it made in the '70s and '80s. *The Washington Post*. Retrieved from https://www.washingtonpost.com/arts-entertainment/2019/10/14/disney-spent-day-reminding-us-truly-bizarre-films-it-made-s-early-s/

Andreychuk, E. (2005). *American frontiersmen on film and television: Boone, Crockett, Bowie, Houston, Bridger and Carson*. Jefferson, NC: McFarland & Company, Inc.

Beaty, B. (2016). Superhero fan service: Audience strategies in the contemporary interlinked Hollywood blockbuster. *The Information Society*, *32*(5), 318–325.

Biskind, P. (1998). *Easy riders, raging bulls*. New York: Simon & Schuster.

Brookey, R., & Gray J. (2017). "Not merely para": Continuing steps in paratextual research. *Critical Studies in Media Communication*, *34*(2), 101–110.

Carrington, A. (2019). From blaxploitation to fan service: Watching Wakanda. *Safundi: The Journal of South African and American Studies*, *20*(1), 5–8.

Clark, T. (2021, Jan. 14). 'The Mandalorian' finally beat 'The Office' as the most watched streaming series in the US, according to Nielsen. *Insider*. Retrieved from https://www.businessinsider.com/mandalorian-tops-nielsen-list-of-most-watched-streaming-tv-shows-2021-1

Couch, A., Siegel, T., & Kit, B. (2021, February 16). Behind Disney's firing of 'Mandalorian' Star Gina Carano. *The Hollywood Reporter*. Retrieved from https://www.hollywoodreporter.com/heat-vision/behind-disneys-firing-of-mandalorian-star-gina-carano

Donaldson, M. (2022, May 31). Obi-Wan proves Star Wars has a Grogu obsession. *Screen Rant*. Retrieved from https://screenrant.com/obi-wan-kenobi-star-wars-grogu-copy-problem/

Epstein, E. (2018, April 15). Internet fandom is running Hollywood. *Quartz*. Retrieved from https://qz.com/quartzy/1207341/fan-service/

Fiske, J. (1987). *Television culture*. London: Methuen & Co.

Fleming, M. (2020, August 2). Tom Pollock's legacy: Lawyered Hollywood's greatest deal, the one that gave George Lucas 'Star Wars' sequel rights. *Deadline*. Retrieved from https://deadline.com/2020/08/tom-pollock-legacy-architect-hollywood-greatest-deal-george-lucas-star-wars-sequel-rights-1203001950/

Gartenberg, C. (2020, January 17). Disney is hunting down the most popular Baby Yoda toys on Esty. *The Verge*. Retrieved from https://www.theverge.com/2020/1/17/ 21069124/baby-yoda-dolls-etsy-disney-mandalorian-copyright-takedown-enforcement

Genette, G. (1997). *Paratexts: Thresholds of interpretation*. (J. E. Lewin, Trans.). Cambridge, UK: Cambridge: Cambridge University Press.

Govindarajan, V. (2016, June 3). How Disney found its way back to creative success. *Harvard Business Review*. Retrieved from https://hbr.org/2016/06/how-disney-found-its-way-back-to-creative-success

Hahn, D. (Director). (2009). *Waking sleeping beauty* (Motion Picture). Burbank, CA: Walt Disney Studios.

Hall, S. (1973). *Encoding and decoding in the television discourse*. Birmingham: Centre for Contemporary Cultural Studies.

Haring, B. (2021, January 20). Disney's Robert Iger praises new Democratic Presidential team in tweet. *Deadline*. Retrieved from https://deadline.com/2021/01/disney-robert-iger-praises-new-presidential-team-1234677439/

Higgins, B. (2019, December 25). Hollywood flashback: The 'Star Wars' holiday special got past George Lucas in 1978. *The Hollywood Reporter.* Retrieved from https://www.hollywoodreporter.com/news/hollywood-flashback-star-wars-holiday-special-got-past-george-lucas-1978-1263309

Idato, M. (2019, November 29). The Mandalorian is edge-of-your-seat thrilling. *The Sydney Morning Herald.* Retrieved from https://www.smh.com.au/culture/tv-and-radio/the-good-the-bad-and-the-bounty-20191121-p53cwt.html

Jenkins, H (2006). Convergence culture: Where old and new media collide. New York: New York University Press.

Kane, G. (1999). Seeing racism in Jar Jar is seeing phantom menace. *The Baltimore Sun.* Retrieved from https://www.baltimoresun.com/news/bs-xpm-1999-06-05-9906050180-story.html

Katz, B. (2020, August 6). Here's how much money Disney's 'Star Wars' films actually earned. *Observer.* Retrieved from https://observer.com/2020/08/star-wars-gross-profit-earningsdisney-box-office/

Kring-Schreifels, J. (2019, November 8). How Boba Fett became a 'Star Wars' icon. *The Ringer.* Retrieved from https://www.theringer.com/movies/2019/11/8/20953924/star-wars-boba-fett-design-the-mandalorian

Kristeva, J. (1980). Desire in language: A semiotic approach to literature and art. New York: Columbia University Press.

Kuchera, B. (2015, January 5). Watch Boba Fett's first ever appearance, and a subtle detail from Empire Strikes Back. *Polygon.* Retrieved from https://www.polygon.com/2015/1/5/7494933/star-wars-boba-fett-animated

Lambie, R. (2019, June 26). Exploring Disney's fascinating dark phase of the 70s and 80s. *Den of Geek.* Retrieved from https://www.denofgeek.com/movies/exploring-disneys-fascinating-dark-phase-of-the-70s-and-80s/

McFarland, M. (2019, December 28). A new hope for "Star Wars" in "The Mandalorian" season finale. *Salon.* Retrieved from https://www.salon.com/2019/12/27/a-new-hope-the-mandalorian-finds-redemption-for-star-wars-in-its-season-finale/

McGloin, M. (2020, July 21). George Lucas saving Star Wars; Kathleen Kennedy leaving for J.J. Abrams. *Cosmic Book New.* Retrieved from https://cosmicbook.news/george-lucas-saving-star-wars-kathleen-kennedy-jj-abrams

Ott, B., & Walter, C. (2000). Intertextuality: Interpretive practice and textual strategy. *Critical Studies in Media Communication*, *17*(4), 429–446.

Radaway, J. (1984). *Reading the romance.* Chapel Hill, NC: University of North Carolina Press.

Ratcliffe, A. (2014, August 28). How the 501st and rebel legions became part of Star Tours. *Star Wars.* Retrieved from https://www.starwars.com/news/how-the-501st-and-rebel-legions-became-part-of-star-tours

Robey, T. (2015, December 14). 10 films that influenced Star Wars. *The Telegraph.* Retrieved from https://www.telegraph.co.uk/film/star-wars--a-new-hope/movies-influences-george-lucas/

Russell, J. (2012, October 31). *Star Wars*: Why Disney was destined to buy Lucasfilm. *The Guardian.* Retrieved from https://www.theguardian.com/film/filmblog/2012/oct/31/star-wars-disney-destined-lucasfilm

Russell, S. (2020, January 30). Baby Yoda: Which animals 'voice' The Mandalorian's breakout star. *CBR.* Retrieved from https://www.cbr.com/baby-yoda-animals-voice-the-mandalorian/

Schwartzel, E., & Watson, R.T. (2019, December 6). Disney disturbs the force: Pleasing Star Wars fans complicates the saga. *The Wall Street Journal*. Retrieved from https://www.wsj.com/articles/the-dark-side-of-disneys-star-wars-bet-11575663914
Scolari, C. (2013). Lostology: Transmedia storytelling and expansion/compression strategies. *Semiotica, 195*(1), 45–68.
Shop Disney. (n.d.). *Shop Disney*. Retrieved from https://www.shopdisney.com/the-child-plush-star-wars-the-mandalorian-small-11-412319525875.html?isProductSearch=0&plpPosition=17&guestFacing=Characters-Star%2520Wars-The%2520Child
Thomas, B. (1994). *An American original: Walt Disney*. Glendale, CA: Disney Editions.
Thorne, W. (2020, November 27). 'The Mandalorian': What's Ahsoka Tan been up to? Baby Yoda's big reveal and more burning questions from 'The Jedi.' *Variety*. Retrieved from https://variety.com/2020/tv/news/the-mandalorian-ahsoka-tano-rasario-dawson-baby-yoda-real-name-the-jedi-recap-1234841143/
Trepany, C. (2021, March 9). Disney CEO responds to Gina Carano 'Mandalorian' controversy, talks 'values that are universal.' *USA Today*. Retrieved from https://www.usatoday.com/story/entertainment/tv/2021/03/09/gina-carano-disney-ceo-says-company-has-no-political-bias/6927712002/
Vary, A. (2021, March 16). 'Star Wars': Ewoks TV movies, Boba Fett 'Holiday Special' debut finally coming to Disney Plus. *Variety*. Retrieved from https://variety.com/2021/tv/news/star-wars-holiday-special-boba-fett-ewoks-caravan-of-courage-disney-plus-1234932286/
Vasquez, Z. (2019, December 3). Big deal he is: How Baby Yoda became 2019's biggest character. *The Guardian*. Retrieved from https://www.theguardian.com/tv-and-radio/2019/dec/03/baby-yoda-the-mandalorian-star-wars
Venable, N. (2019, Nov. 21). How The Mandalorian kept Baby Yoda a secret from Star Wars fans. *Cinemablend*. Retrieved from https://www.cinemablend.com/television/2485357/how-the-mandalorian-kept-baby-yoda-a-secret-from-star-wars-fans
Wasko, J. (2001). *Understanding Disney* (1st ed.). Malden, MA: Polity.
Yasharoff, H. (2021, February 21). Gina Carano says Disney 'bullied' her after controversial posts: 'I'm going to go down swinging.' *USA Today*. Retrieved from: https://www.usatoday.com/story/entertainment/tv/2021/02/21/gina-carano-ousted-mandalorian-star-says-disney-bullied-her/4533378001/

5 The Wonderful World of Jeff Goldblum

When Walt Disney began pitching show ideas to the television networks in the early 1950s, the anthology format was already well established in this relatively new medium. Disney's interest in the format was specific to the company's interests because the flexibility of the genre would allow for the promotion of both the Disneyland Park and its new film offerings. This format would also allow Walt Disney to step in as host and position himself as the primary brand ambassador for the company. Ultimately, this decision became very strategic, and with the cultivation of the "Uncle Walt" persona, Disney became a welcome guest in television households (Capodagli & Jackson, 1999). *The Disneyland Story* debuted on the ABC (American Broadcasting Company) network in 1954. In addition to promoting the park, the show also previewed the live-action film *20,000 Leagues Under the Sea* (1954). Through the years, this anthology program would go through name changes (including becoming *Walt Disney Presents* in 1958 and *Walt Disney's Wonderful World of Color* in 1961) and change networks, but Walt was a constant presence on the show until his death in 1966 (Cotter, 1997). The show also proved to be successful with audiences. Although it experienced a dip in ratings after Disney's death, it continued until its cancelation in 1983. Michel Eisner, however, would revive the anthology series, airing first on ABC as *The Disney Sunday Movie* (1986) before moving to NBC as *The Magical World of Disney* (1988), and then finally landing on The Disney Channel.

The fact that the term "world" would so often appear in the title of the various iterations of this anthology series is worthy of note. It established a broad scope for the series, and it positioned Walt as the man who would introduce audiences to this "world." Sandwiched between the promotional segments and those that repurposed Disney's content, there were nature documentary segments that explored remote parts of the world (the Antarctic, for example) and took the audience to view wildlife in Africa and South America (Cotter, 1997). In these segments, audiences were invited to view a world brought to them by Walt Disney and a perspective that was decidedly Walt's.

DOI: 10.4324/9781003364658-5

Disney's anthology shows positioned nature and adventure segments as a standard staple of the company brand in fundamental ways. After it had acquired the assets of 21st Century Fox, Disney was looking to incorporate the content of the acquisition into the Disney+ service, and the National Geographic brand was a reasonable choice. The content found under the National Geographic section of the service includes sub-sections with titles such as "Explore our World," "Ancient Mysteries," and "Nat Geo Kids." Among the original programming offered is a show entitled *Magic of Disney's Animal Kingdom* (2020), with different episodes that take viewers behind the scenes of Disney World's "animal experiences." Given that this show is also under the National Geographic brand, the Disney+ synergistic practices are firmly in place.

However, our attention in this chapter will be directed toward another Disney+/National Geographic original offering: *The World According to Jeff Goldblum*. As the title suggests, this show takes its cue from Disney's anthology show. Although Goldblum's persona is decidedly different from Uncle Walt's, there is a fundamental similarity; both shows invite the viewer to experience the world from the perspective of not only a middle-aged white man, but also a major media conglomerate. This perspective is not necessarily wholly inaccurate, but it is specific and thin in its rendering of other cultures. This chapter will argue that *The World According to Jeff Goldblum* offers viewers one thin rendering after another. In each episode, Goldblum explores everyday objects and items and invests them with significant weight. In the first season, he explored sneakers, ice cream, bikes, and coffee (to name just a few examples) and traces their origins and broader cultural implications. For its second season, Mr. Goldblum invested in areas that would make Uncle Walt proud, such as magic, birthdays, and backyards. While Goldblum may uncover a thorny issue in his explorations, those concerns are often dismissed at the conclusion of each episode when he discovers what he imagines to be the essential truth about the object or item in question.

While the concept of orientalism (Said, 1978) would be appropriate to an analysis of *The World According to Jeff Goldblum*, we feel that the critical engagement of cosmopolitanism is a more helpful construct. Although generally cosmopolitanism has been regarded as a means of increasing cultural understanding and acceptance, when it is tied to consumptive practices, media consumption in particular, significant problems arise. For example, Carla Jones and Ann Marie Leshkowich (2003) observe how cultural differences can be commodified in a manner they describe as "homogenized heterogeneity," in which those differences are unimportant to the global unity propagated by modernity. A prime example would be Disney's iconic "It's a Small World" ride, first introduced at the 1964–1965 New York World's Fair, then later installed at the Disney parks. Although the ride seems to represent cultural differences, all the characters in the ride are of a uniform size and shape, and the song actually celebrates sameness: "there's so much that we share that it's time we're aware, it's a small world after all." While the ride introduces diverse cultures, the song invites the rider/viewer to regard those differences as immaterial to all the things "that we share." Given that this ride was introduced to television audiences through Disney's anthology show, the commodification of cultural difference is endemic to the Disney brand.

Admittedly, Jeff Goldblum is no Walt Disney. Yet, his anthology show invites the viewer to see the world through his perspective, and the Disney brand decidedly informs that perspective. This chapter will provide an analysis of *The World According to Jeff Goldblum* to illustrate how the perspective is manifest and argue that it evokes cosmopolitanism in a politically insidious manner. We begin with the history of 21st Century Fox and its collaboration with National Geographic, and its acquisition by Disney. We then provide a review of the literature on the commodification of cosmopolitanism, focusing on the concept of "banal cosmopolitanism," and explain how we see the concept refigured in the show. Then we apply this refigured concept to the various episodes of the first season.

Fox, National Geographic, and Disney

The origins of 21st Century Fox studios can be traced back to 1904 when William Fox (formerly Vimos Fried) purchased a 'nickelodeon,' an early movie theater concept, in Brooklyn. Fox made a lot of money as a film exhibitionist, and in order to expand his growing company, he turned to the film production and distribution business. There was one big problem with doing this – The Motion Picture Patents Company, a trust made up of ten film producers and distributors. This trust owned most of the patents for cameras and projectors and was able to restrict the supply of raw film stock to its licensees. The trust also restricted the length of films to a maximum of two reels or 20 minutes. Fox refused to sell to the monopoly and sued using the Sherman Antitrust Act as his rationale. The courts ruled against the monopoly, and from this point on, the film business was open to all (Solomon, 2002).

Fox kept expanding his empire by purchasing more theaters, many of them former vaudeville houses. His "Fox Metropolitan" theaters expanded, and by 1927 he owned over 1,000 nationwide (Solomon, 2002). Fox purchased land and built Movietone City, a 100-acre facility that included space for producing talking pictures. Also, the Fox company looked at expansion overseas, and the opportunity to move into the European market gave the company a chance to expand. Fox succeeded in setting up distribution companies in nearly every major European city (Solomon, 2002).

This aggressive expansion, however, would also be Fox's undoing. In 1927, one of his rivals, Marcus Loew, died. Loew's, Inc. owned Metro-Goldwyn-Mayer with Louis B. Mayer as its president, along with more than 200 theaters nationwide. Fox wanted to buy control of Loew's by purchasing Nicholas Schenck's shares in the company that he ran as president. When Mayer got wind of the deal, he asked the US Department of Justice to investigate. It just so happened that Mayer was connected to the US President Herbert Hoover's administration. In the interim, Fox moved forward and took out loans to purchase Loew's, and he also paid $20 million to purchase the Poli theaters in New England (Solomon, 2002). In October of 1929, the stock market crashed, and the Great Depression began. Fox's dream of buying Loew's died. The loans came due in late 1929 and 1930. The entities that loaned him the money wanted to sell off Fox and split up its assets. Fox's creditors, who had little empathy for him, based on the way he treated people, would not give him any more money. Further complicating the situation was an anti-trust suit that the US brought against the company for the proposed merger with Loew's (Solomon, 2002). In his almost seven-year battle, Fox attempted to bribe the judge but was arrested and convicted, and he served time in prison in 1942 for this deed (Velkey, 2016).

Because of these legal and financial problems, Fox lost control of the studio and was ousted from his position in 1930. In 1935, Fox Film Corporation merged with Twentieth Century Pictures, and 20th Century Fox was born. Sidney Kent became the president of the merged company, and Darryl F. Zanuck was named vice-president in charge of production, a position he would hold until 1971 (except for 1956 to 1961when he worked as an independent producer). During Zanuck's tenure, the studio would have both hits (*The Sound of Music,* 1965) and misses (*Cleopatra*, 1963). Arguably the studio's biggest hit came after Zanuck's departure when *Star Wars* was released to theaters in 1977. The success of this film and the resulting franchise helped quadruple the company's stock price. This financial stability allowed 20th Century Fox to move forward and create content for its various branches while continuing to diversify its assets. In 1981, a team headed by Marc Rich and Marvin Davis purchased the company for $700 million. In 1984, Rich ran off to Switzerland after being charged with tax evasion, racketeering, and illegal trading with Iran during the hostage crisis. Davis ended up buying out Rich's interest in 20th Century Fox and took control of the company (Hayes, 1984).

In 1985, however, Rupert Murdoch stepped into the picture. As head of News Corporation, the Australian-born Murdoch was looking to get into the US media market. For context, the Federal Communication Commission (FCC) did not allow non-US citizens to own broadcast properties. Because of this legality, Mr. Murdoch became a US citizen. He then purchased a stake in 20th Century Fox from Marvin Davis. Murdoch's ownership was the beginning of a massive uptick in purchases of media outlets in America and subsequent consolidation in the media industry. Murdoch also bought the Metromedia television stations from entrepreneur John Kluge, which served as the initial building blocks for the Fox television network. Murdoch then bought out Marvin Davis' remaining stake in 20th Century Fox for $325 million (Wolff, 2010). Rupert Murdoch now owned a US-based film and television company and a group-owned television station network that he would use to create the Fox Television Network in 1986 (Wolff, 2010).

In the following years, Murdoch spent considerable capital building up his News Corp. brand. He launched the Fox News Channel, expanded Sky TV in Europe, created STAR TV for Asia, consolidated his assets under his news and magazine publications, and kept growing the film division. In 1997 Fox and National Geographic partnered to create The National Geographic cable channel, which launched in 2001. The channel was intended to deliver high-quality, nonfiction programming under the National Geographic banner, including documentaries, nature shows, and science shows, and cultural, historical, and entertainment programming with a scientific twist. Although there were significant differences between these two media organizations, the partnership seemed to work. Other National Geographic branded channels were launched. This partnership would end when Fox took over all National Geographic's assets, including the venerable magazine, in 2015 in a $725 million acquisition deal (Thielman, 2015).

To respond to a changing media market, Rupert Murdoch announced in 2012 that News Corp. would be split into two companies – one for publishing and one for media. He announced that 20th Century Fox would now be 21st Century Fox to better align with where the company was going while preserving its founding heritage. The publishing arm would continue to be under the News Corp. umbrella. However, Murdoch knew that even Fox's remaining businesses would be disrupted by digital distribution and knew the time was right to sell. According to Robert Iger's (2019) biography, Murdoch approached Disney about acquiring Fox. After a battle with Comcast, Verizon Communications, and Sony, The Walt Disney Company purchased 20th Century Fox and other 21st Century Fox holdings for approximately $71.3 billion. Disney secured 20th Century Fox, Fox Searchlight Pictures, the FX cable channels, Fox's TV production company, control of Hulu, a massive library of classic films, franchises, and of course, National Geographic (Sims, 2019). The purchase did not include the Fox broadcast network, the Fox Sports channels, or the Fox News or Fox Business channels to satisfy anti-trust concerns.

The acquisition was historic in that a film studio with a 100-year history has all but disappeared from the media landscape. On January 17, 2020, *Variety* reported that Disney was dropping the "Fox" name from all the assets it has acquired, with the succinct lead: "The mouse has officially killed the fox" (Vary, 2020, p. 1). Disney saw the acquisition as an opportunity to add more content to its portfolio in anticipation of the roll-out of Disney+ (Iger, 2019). As we mentioned earlier, Disney's control of Hulu allows it to place content inappropriate for Disney on a different streaming service; for example, shows from the FX channels will appear on Hulu. Finally, Disney can draw on Fox's back catalog of films and television shows and place those properties on either Hulu or Disney+ in the future. The purchase of Fox also brings several Marvel characters back under Disney's control of Marvel Cinematic Universe (MCU). In addition to the X-Men and the Fantastic Four, Disney regains the film rights to The Hulk and Deadpool. Now, Disney has more latitude to incorporate both Deadpool and X-Men into the *Avengers* film series' timeline and develop their standalone works as part of the MCU, and as we have noted, this universe has prospered under Disney's ownership.

When the Disney acquisition of Fox was announced, leadership at National Geographic viewed the development very favorably. In a 2019 interview with the financial times, Courteney Monroe, CEO of National Geographic television Global Networks, describes how the brand had been undermined by programming that was seeking to compete with both The History Channel and the Discovery Channel. She felt that the Disney acquisition would bode well for National Geographic: "Disney is going to enable us to turbocharge our business. . . We have a creatively ambitious vision for our programming, and we do have bigger budgets, we're taking bigger, bolder swings" (Harvey, 2019, p. 7).

Among the bigger swings was the launch of Disney+, as National Geographic figured prominently on the streaming service interface as one of the primary content areas. One of the first National Geographic shows that premiered with the launch of the service was the Disney+ original *The World According to Jeff Goldblum*. Jeff Goldblum is an American television actor known primarily for his roles in the original *Jurassic Park* (1993) movies along with a remake of *The Fly* (1986) and on TV with *Law and Order: Criminal Intent* (2001). Goldblum is also known for his quirky personality and highly intelligent persona, qualities that are fully displayed in the program. As we mentioned earlier, each episode allows Goldblum to explore a particular object or topic, and his quirkiness is on full display during his investigations. These explorations take Goldblum to various locales, and in this way, the show also becomes a travelog that fits neatly within the National Geographic brand.

The show's reviews have been mixed, although generally favorable, with a *Rotten Tomatoes* aggregate critics score of 82% ("The World According," n.d.). Writing for *The Hollywood Reporter*, Daniel Feinberg stated,

> As a purely educational experience, 'The World According to Jeff Goldblum' is only a limited success. Goldblum is boundlessly interested, but he is not a reporter. He seemingly has not been fed an agenda of inquiries, so his interviews tend toward enthusiasm instead of an interrogation. The animated historical segments tend to stick to a two-sentence summary of information. It is relatively easy to come away from an episode feeling like on a fact-by-fact level, you gleaned little.
>
> (Feinberg, 2019, para. 11)

We find this assessment interesting because the show's episodes are packed with a variety of facts regarding the subject matter, but we agree that the ultimate takeaway from the various episodes seems a bit slight. Dustin Rowles, the publisher of *Pajiba*, sums up the problem succinctly:

> The logline for the series promises "astonishing connections, fascinating science, and a whole lot of big ideas," but in the first episode, Jeff Goldblum mostly marvels at how expensive sneakers are. . . Goldblum essentially takes us through the life of a sneaker, from its creation to its purchase to its unboxing, and the only "big idea" behind the first episode, anyway, seems to be "capitalism."
>
> (Rowles, 2019, para. 4)

This sleight-of-hand, offering several points of significant connection while offering little significance, brings us back to the discussion of cosmopolitanism, and more specifically, banal cosmopolitanism.

Making the Banal Cosmopolitan

As we mentioned earlier, the critical literature on cosmopolitanism has identified problems with global media commercialization, and those problems can often be located in the global media practices of Disney. For our purposes, we would like to focus on a form of cosmopolitanism that has emerged from this literature, banal cosmopolitanism. The concept of banal cosmopolitanism was first posited by Ulrich Beck (2004) to describe a perspective that emerges from the consumptive experiences that connect cultures and cross-national boundaries. He sees this perspective as the product of mediated globalization and argues that cosmopolitanism has become a commodity in the global media marketplace. Consequently, media scholars have found Beck's concept valuable in the critical engagement of global media forms. For example, in his analysis of the video game *FIFA World Cup 2010*, Andrew Baerg (2015) argues that design mechanics of the game present players with a perspective that, while inviting identification with the teams from other countries, does not invite an engagement of the cultural or political contexts of those countries.

Giselinde Kuipers and Jeroen de Kloet (2009) have studied audience reception of the film *The Lord of the Rings: Return of the King* (2003), and their findings are also instructive of the concept of banal cosmopolitanism. In their study, they surveyed over 24,000 respondents from 150 countries, and they found that audiences responded to the film in surprisingly uniform ways. As they conclude:

> The cultural industry capitalizes on – and creates – the wish of audiences to experience globality in their everyday lives. Our discovery of identical or similar modes of reception of The Lord of the Rings in

> various countries inspired us to label it as an exemplary case of banal cosmopolitanism. The diverse decodings of the LotR text by audiences worldwide do not signal the emergence of a pan-national media sphere in which culturally diverse audiences creatively decode and appropriate cultural products. Rather, we suggest that these diverse decodings are to some extent orchestrated and "encoded" by international media conglomerates.
>
> (2009, p. 116)

Given Disney's global reach, it shares the same motives as WarnerMedia (now part of Warner Bros. Discovery), owner of New Line Cinema, the production company for the film, to create a homogeneous experience. In fact, as we pointed out earlier in our reference to the "It's a Small World" ride, Disney has been in the business of taking international cultural forms and rendering them down to a singular experience for several decades.

Beck offers a warning about the impact of banal cosmopolitanism on contemporary consciousness:

> What counts as national is, in its essence, increasingly transnational or cosmopolitan. Hence, the relationship between our cognitive understanding of the world and the actual social structures is becoming paradoxical: social structures and processes become cosmopolitan, while our knowledge remains caught up in national axioms. It seems likely, moreover, that economic and cultural globalization will tend to strengthen rather than weaken this paradox of knowledge and reality.
>
> (2004, p. 153)

We see this warning as prescient, particularly where *The World According to Jeff Goldblum* is concerned.

While the show takes on the form of a travelog anthology (reflecting established television offerings of both Disney and National Geographic), uncovering a variety of facts about otherwise unremarkable artifacts, and positioning them in a broader historical and global context, those contexts are very carefully edited. In other words, while the show seems to make the banal cosmopolitan, that cosmopolitan perspective is in the end banal. More to the point, the show either dismisses or ignores the more problematic aspects of these objects, particularly in relation to their production and consumption. Instead, the show presents these objects in a way that asserts elements of the Disney style, particularly in relation to innocence and optimism. We will highlight those elements in the analysis that follows, but we will also identify the rather insidious way the show tries to render the banal cosmopolitan, but in a way that also renders political and cultural issues immaterial. In addition, we also note how Goldblum concludes each episode with a summation of his findings, one that reasserts a universal and homogenized worldview. In other words, *The World According to Jeff*

Goldblum may reside under the National Geographic label, but it is, in the final analysis, a Disney product.

What a Wonderful World, Mostly

As we have mentioned, *The World According to Jeff Goldblum* is an anthology show, not unlike the early Disney programs. Goldblum, of course, projects a persona that is decidedly different from Walt Disney's, although he expresses the same childlike wonder that Disney was skilled at projecting to audiences. In each episode, Goldblum explores a different, ordinary subject or object. While these explorations may uncover some uncomfortable truths (the environmental impact of the manufacture of jeans, for example), these truths are often swiftly abandoned as Goldblum moves on with his exploration. The purpose of this show is not to offer hard-hitting journalism but programming in the style associated with the Disney brand, and to provide audiences with a positive message about otherwise ordinary objects. Consequently, the program goes against a more balanced documentary style, often associated with National Geographic's programs, and instead is a Walt Disney Company project through and through. In the analysis that follows, we examine some of the episodes of the first season of the series and look at how the "Disney touch" has been added to the show.

In season one, episode three, titled "Tattoos," Goldblum explores the world of this art form and how it has become mainstream. His goal is to find the "deeper meaning of tattoos." He travels to Baltimore to attend a tattoo convention. As he walks through the convention floor, he talks to the camera, addressing the audience directly as Walt Disney used to do. Goldblum mentions his Jewish heritage and how his aversion to tattoos was informed by an understanding of the experience of the Holocaust. One would think that this point would lead to a deeper dive into this sensitive topic. After all, there are deeper and darker meanings of tattoos, particularly those depicting hatred based on race, sexual orientation, and gender identity. Goldblum offers his statement about tattoos and the Holocaust in one sentence and moves on. There is no further mention of this through the rest of the program.

Instead, Goldblum's exploration attempts to define tattoos in ways that oppose them to the purposes they had in fascist regimes. After attending the tattoo convention and talking to the attendees, Goldblum observes that tattooing is about "ownership of our own bodies," although he wonders if there is a deeper motivation. This question brings him to Hawaii, and here he investigates the significance of tattooing in the Kanaka Maoli culture. He observes the ancient practices of tattooing (which are decidedly low-tech) and interviews several people who have traditional tattoos. They talk about how it identifies them and tells their story, and how in some cases, they overcame challenges. For example, Archie Kalepa explains how his tattoo symbolizes a near-death experience he had while surfing and claims the tattoo reminds him to be observant of the world around him. By highlighting the positive aspects of tattooing, the program glosses over the negative aspects. Indeed, at the conclusion of the program, Goldblum determines that tattooing is about "affirmation and something that might be called self-definition," which is decidedly different than their uses to identify those subjected to the Holocaust. In other words, tattooing is about asserting individualism.

It is important to note how these conclusions are offered to the audience and framed by the program. Each episode follows Goldblum as he explores an object, and his conclusion is presented as emerging from what he has learned during his exploration. In addition, the conclusion is framed as an articulation of deeper meaning surrounding said object. Therefore, when Goldblum concludes that tattoos are about affirmation and self-definition, this conclusion is offered as an essential truth. All other related truths are secondary at best, including those associated with the Holocaust. For example, Hawaii Public Radio interviewed another Hawaiian citizen, Nick Ochs, the leader of the O'ahu chapter of the Proud Boys. In the interview, Ochs repeats and supports the disparaging remarks Trump has made about other countries and cultures. In the photo accompanying the story, he proudly displays his Proud Boy tattoo (Tanigawa, 2018). In other words, in the same state Goldblum discovered the truth about tattoos, another truth revealed how an assertion of individualism could be an act of nullification, and as we learned on January 6, 2021, related to abject violence.

In an episode devoted to denim, Goldblum begins by pointing out that denim is worn by half of the global population at any given time. How this fact is established is not disclosed. However, it illustrates the banality of the fabric while also asserting it as an object with a global presence. Indeed, his exploration uncovers the cosmopolitan history of denim. He begins by explaining how the cotton plant originated in Africa, the seeds of which migrated around the globe. In Nimes, France, cotton fabric was first called De Nimes, which over time has become "denim." In the US, we learn Jacob Davis used copper rivets to strengthen the denim trousers for a particular client. As Goldblum explains, Davis went into business with Levi Strauss, and the iconic brand of jeans was born. Later in the episode, the history of indigo dye is traced back "6,000 years ago to Peru." Goldblum explains that the dye on denim is built up in layers that are then worn down so that each pair of jeans "becomes as individual as a fingerprint."

The episode also discloses that the industrial practices of producing denim are notoriously polluting and consume unsustainable amounts of water. These problems have been well documented (Chico, Aldaya & Garrido, 2013). We would add that there are also significant labor problems related to the manufacture of jeans, especially the manual labor that goes into sanding and destressing jeans (Claudio, 2007). Goldblum, however, visits Bart Sights, a "VP of Tech Innovation" for Levi Strauss, who claims to be addressing these problems with technology, specifically lasers.

We are then shown how designs, and even rips and tears, can be burned into jeans using a laser device and computer interface. Goldblum tells us that "Bart and his team with their high-tech tools are aiming to clean up the whole denim world, somewhat." After Goldblum picks out a design, we are shown how the laser slowly pans the jeans and burns the design into the fabric. Sights shows us how jeans were manufactured "a couple of years ago," and in a video on his iPad, he reveals we are seeing about "800 men in a room, repetitive motion, least desirable jobs in the factory," acknowledging the labor issues related to the industry. Sights then "fast forwards" to today, and we are shown the process being completed with lasers. Admittedly the image shows a cleaner, less cluttered work environment, with only two people working, and we are told that this process "only uses a fraction of the chemicals and creates much less waste." It is also clear from the picture that the process produces a fraction of the jeans produced by the older methods. We are told that Sights' process produces "over 3,000 different styles of jeans every season," but as Luz Claudio (2007) has noted, the manufacture of distressed jeans in a Chinese factory can produce 10,000 pairs a day. This puts into perspective Goldblum's earlier "somewhat" qualification.

Ultimately, the episode reproduces one of Disney's well-worn optimistic tropes; technology can solve problems. Indeed, Walt Disney's original design of EPCOT (Experimental Prototype Community of Tomorrow) was focused on how technology would overcome the problems of urbanization. Those plans were abandoned to add another theme park in Disney World (Knight, 2014). While this episode explores the international history and impact of denim, the negative aspects of that impact are held up as problems of the past that will be solved with the technology of the future. As for the jeans themselves, Goldblum concludes that they allow the wearer to assert individuality (not unlike tattoos), but in an essentially authentic manner. "Authenticity," he states, "that's it in a nutshell, and I think I'm done here." With that, Goldblum also dismisses any issues related to labor practices and the environment.

Technology also figures prominently in the episode on gaming. Goldblum starts off this episode by playing *Ms. Pac Man* (1982) and avers that "gaming has evolved" and invites us to join him as he "discovers a brave new digital world that has turned into a cultural phenomenon." He begins at an esports tournament for the game *Counter-Strike* (2000). He meets with Vitality, a team from France, and watches as they compete against, and lose to, a team from Brazil. So early in the episode we are introduced to the international reach of esports. After the match, Goldblum gives a brief history of video gaming, beginning in 1958 with the invention of the game "Tennis for Two." He quickly moves through the introduction of *Pong* (1972) in the 1970s and the emergence of Nintendo in the 1980s. He then describes the video game industry as a "technological arms race for bigger and better games."

It is at this point in the episode when an interesting segue occurs. Goldblum visits Moonwalk Audio, a sound design company for the video game industry. The audio designers show Goldblum some of the work they have done on *Wonka's World of Candy* (2018), a mobile game spinoff of the famous film that even incorporates the likeness of Gene Wilder. We are then shown the designers creating foley sound effects for the game; a practice originated to create sound effects for film. In fact, the designers explain that sound design for gaming is remarkably similar to sound design practices for film. We see Goldblum explore the connection between the film and video game industries, a connection that has been well established (Brookey, 2010). Indeed, Disney has been incredibly involved in developing video games from their film content, so it is a connection that promotes the practices of the company.

This connection and promotion of Disney's practices are extended, albeit indirectly, when Goldblum delves into the world of live-action role-playing (LARP). LARP participants dress in costumes and assume character roles to act out in real-time and in a constructed environment (in this case, a medieval village). As one of the participants explains, it mixes improvisational theater and sport. Goldblum participates and is escorted through an angry mob, not unlike *The Hunchback of Notre Dame* (which happens to be a 1996 Disney animated movie based on the novel by Victor Hugo). At the end of their journey, Mr. Goldblum stirs the crowd with a speech, but an assassin comes up and tries to kill him. The assassin fails and is killed within the LARP game. When Goldblum inquires as to the connection between LARPing and video gameplay, one of the participants opines, "here you get to actually feel like you are in the world, you are fully immersed in it, and you are living your character."

This harkens to the Disney theme parks where actors perform as Disney characters and "LARP" with the guests visiting the park. Indeed, the theme park experiences and rides are tied to narratives that invite the guest to LARP. The guest can pretend to be magically transported into the different worlds imagined by Disney's film and television products. In addition, like the theme park, the LARPing in which Goldblum participates is safe, and the good folks always win in the end – the Disney brand inside a gaming environment. Therefore, Goldblum's exploration of video gaming connects the practice to the film industry and the immersive experience of the theme park, thereby indirectly promoting principal elements of the Disney corporation. One could argue that this connection overlaps into season two where Goldblum explores birthdays (always an essential element of the park experience), backyards (what says Americana more than the backyard), and fireworks (yet another key element in the Disney parks).

After his LARPing experience, Goldblum acknowledges the complaints brought against video gaming, particularly the depiction of violence and the alienation of gameplay. Yet, Goldblum takes this opportunity to provide a rebuttal to the claims made against video gaming. For example, he remarks that while there are "new reports that say gaming is creating a generation that is sleepwalking through life," there is also research that indicates gaming not only keeps the brain active but also may increase the size of certain areas of the brain. Regarding the concerns that video gameplay is isolating, Goldblum avers that gaming creates virtual communities that allow people to connect across the globe.

While it is true that communities and cultures have formed around gaming, those communities sometimes carry malevolent intent. Studies of the #Gamergate conflict have explored how sexism is present in gaming culture and how women gamers have been subject to violent threats (Massanari, 2017). Other studies have illustrated how racism can also inform these gaming communities (Brookey & Ecenbarger, 2016). Then there is the case of Tyler Barriss, who was sentenced to 20 years in federal prison for making a "swatting" call (an erroneous call to police) that resulted in the death of Andrew Finch. This occurred over an argument in an online multiplayer session of *Call of Duty: WWII* (2017), although the victim was not even the target of the swatting as the police were given the wrong address by Barriss (Hanna & Lynch, 2019). Therefore, the communities to which Goldblum refers illustrate that concerns over video gaming culture are not so easily dismissed, but dismiss them he does: "well, bookmark it there, but let's continue the conversation."

That conversation returns to digital technology as Goldblum explores advances in the world of "virtual reality," or VR. This technology transports the participant into a three-dimensional world where they can be "inside" the gaming environment. VR has often been offered up as the next technological wave for the gaming industry. If a successful consumer version of the technology is produced, it could create the next generation of gaming. Goldblum looks at this world with innocence and optimism that imagines an extraordinary experience for the future of gaming. He concludes that "gaming can be a vehicle for our advancement, to the extent that games can be a realization of the wonderful world aspect of life" (sic). Yet, this optimism about technology generally, and gaming technology specifically, is already incorporated into Disney's practices. In addition to the connections to a theme park and film narrative, there is also a connection to production practices. In fact, in another section of Disney+, the potential Goldblum mentions has been realized with the similar virtual world technology used extensively in the production of *The Mandalorian*, which expands upon the Star Wars universe. Specifically, the fourth episode of the *Disney Gallery/Star Wars: The Mandalorian* (which we discussed in the previous chapter) documents how video game technology was used to create the virtual sets for the show. In other words, this technology is already a part of the "wonderful world" of Disney.

The interest in technology also informs the episode devoted to bikes. After watching BMX bikers in action, Goldblum traces the history of the bike back to 1817 with the invention of the velocipede. He then goes to the headquarters of Specialized Bicycle Components, where he learns about how experimental research is incorporated into bike design, including carbon fiber. He also tests out a biking outfit in a wind chamber to demonstrate how clothing design also figures into the technology of bike performance, after which he posits that there is "much more to learn about expertise and innovation." The episode then shifts to discussing how biking has led to various transportation innovations, including the Wright Brothers. They used their expertise in designing bikes to develop early aviation. Henry Ford also used his experience as a bicycle mechanic to develop a motorized quadricycle, which would serve as a precursor for the automobile.

At this point, Goldblum discusses the transition from bikes to the automobile, as we are shown vintage footage of various early automobiles and their manufacture. Goldblum's narration provides a brief summary of the rise and fall of Fordism (Harvey, 1994) as it relates to the auto industry generally and Detroit specifically, mentioning that it "created jobs, booming industry. . . the automobile defined the United States in the 20th Century, and bikes were just a thing of the past. The car, that was the future, until it wasn't." The scene shifts to "Motor City today, a city that broke down when the car industry flatlined," and the camera pans the exterior and interior of abandoned factories to illustrate Goldblum's narration. He suggests, however, that there is some hope for the future of Detroit thanks to the return of the bicycle. The video then shows us ariel shots of people gathering in a park for the beginning of the "Slow Roll." As Goldblum explains, the Slow Roll is a weekly community bike ride through the city of Detroit.

In order to participate, however, Goldblum must find a bicycle, and so he goes to meet Henry Ford (the second) at a bike shop simply called Detroit Bikes. Henry Ford II explains that his dad was also called Henry Ford and worked in the auto industry for Chrysler. However, his family is not part of the more commonly known Ford family. As Goldblum notes, although consumers in the US buy 16 million bikes a year, "one-half of one percent are made here" in the US Detroit Bikes, he observes, "is one of a handful of manufactures here in America. They can produce 150 handcrafted bicycles a day." Henry Ford II explains how he came to manufacture bikes, and his is a story that speaks to the decline of the auto industry in the US. He mentions that he was laid off from the auto industry in 2008 and was looking for work for two years. One day, he noticed a group of kids riding their bikes by his house, which sparked his interest. He then explains how Detroit Bikes hand manufactures bikes with customized designs and features.

In other words, Henry Ford II is offered as an example of post-Fordist production in Detroit, replacing mass production with specialized manufacturing on a smaller, more flexible scale (Harvey, 1994). Therefore, he is offered by Goldblum as signifying the rebirth of Detroit. In the scenes that follow, Goldblum is shown riding the bike created for him by Detroit Bikes. Goldblum then joins the Slow Roll, and we are introduced to the founder of the ride, Mike Mackool. As he explains, the Slow Roll started simply with five or ten people, and now about 3,000–5,000 participate each week.

He also argues that the Slow Roll has had a significant, positive impact on Detroit: "We see people moving back because of the Slow Roll. We see people participating in restaurants and going to different bars and staying in the city once they get here. Which is huge." Goldblum then observes how the car changed our society and our cities' design, not necessarily for the better. Yet, as he notes, "bicycles, of course, have no emissions, so people are claiming their cities back, with bikes helping to make them feel human again." In fact, in his conclusion, he mentions that the ability of the bike to connect a community, "that's no small thing." Although the bike is a mechanism, he feels that the bike that was made for him was an extension of his body. It made him feel connected with his environment. His final words for this episode: "Well, it feels like, in some way, I'm home."

Obviously, this conclusion presents the bicycle as an object with the force to reverse the automobile's negative impact and to revive a city that has come to symbolize the collapse of the auto industry. We would suggest that this invests the bicycle with an overly optimistic force. In this episode, Detroit Bikes and the bicycle is offered as a post-Fordist remedy to the decline of manufacturing, but as David Harvey (1994) has observed, the rise of post-Fordism has also shifted the economic dynamics in ways that have reduced the middle class, increased structural unemployment, and contributed to urban poverty. Pace Henry Ford II and Jeff Goldblum, we do not believe that the return of the bicycle can address those broader social and economic problems, even in Detroit.

The discursive practices of projecting cosmopolitanism in a selective, optimistic light are most pronounced in the episode devoted to jewelry. Goldblum spends time with a Houston, Texas-based jewelry maker, Johnny Dang, who specializes in "grills," a jewel-encrusted cover that goes over the teeth. Goldblum observes how the practice of creating jeweled teeth "can be traced back to at least 2500 B.C., thanks to the discovery of ancient Egyptians who got buried with their gold teeth." He also notes that "around the eighth century A.D., the Mayan put precious stones right into their enamels." Therefore, what seems to be a contemporary practice has a history that crosses centuries and continents. Yet, the negative implications of these practices are quickly dismissed.

When Goldblum meets a rapper (Paul Wall) who claims to have started the trend of wearing grills, he asks the rapper about the class politics of this conspicuous consumption. He does so by offering the question as a hypothetical response from someone who might take umbrage with the practice with the question "shouldn't we equalize the wealth?" Paul Wall answers thusly:

> We definitely should, but my response is, what encouraged me was to see people shining who worked hard for it, went out there and got it. They had adversity, but they overcame it. That's what inspired me to go out and do it. So, hopefully, this will be used as some type of inspiration.

This exchange illustrates the insidious way the show engages and dismisses negative implications. Goldblum's question is offered as a form of mimicry, which undermines the legitimacy of the question. Paul Wall's answer begins by suggesting the question is a legitimate concern, but one that is easily addressed by a conservative work ethic, implicitly suggesting that these extravagant products are available to anyone who is willing to work for them. Perhaps more troubling is the suggestion that this type of consumption is the necessary motivation that people need to succeed and overcome adversity.

What the episode ignores are the conditions of the cultivation of jewels and precious metals. For example, Greg Campbell (2012) provides an extensive historical analysis of the diamond trade. He reveals that they are called "blood diamonds" for a reason. The violent conflicts over the cultivation of these jewels have undermined the country of Sierra Leone and resulted in countless deaths. Richard Saunders (2016) has argued that the diamond industry in Zimbabwe has served to support a political and economic elite class, and has done little to improve the conditions of those outside of these elite groups. In addition, scholars have noted the negative impact of gold mining on the environment and the health of those who do the mining (Ogola, Mitullah & Omulo, 2002). While the episode traces the cultural history of jewelry over a broad swath of time and geography, these conditions of production are ignored.

Instead, Goldblum explores what he sees as the deeper meaning of jewelry, and his exploration leads him to an Indian wedding. What he learns from his investigation of Indian culture is that there is "more to wearing of precious jewels than just showin' off . . . it means something culturally and historically. It's a lovely thing." Indeed, Goldblum offers evidence that the appeal of jewelry can be found in the Paleolithic period among Neanderthals. He also attempts to detach this appeal from material conditions when he visits a group of men who use glitter and plastic jewels as adornment for Southern Decadence, a contemporary gay cultural event in New Orleans. He makes the case that these items empower people, and he concludes: "jewelry isn't necessarily about showin' off how much we can afford to spend, but rather helping the world to see us for who we really are. And that's something upon which we cannot put a price." Except, Johnny Dang does just that at the beginning of the episode when we are told that his grills range in price from \$30,000 to \$250,000. In fact, the death and human suffering that has resulted from the jewelry trade illustrates that the price of empowerment is quite high, and often paid by those most disempowered by the industry.

Goldblum's efforts to explore the deeper meanings and implications of common objects are very selective. As this episode on jewelry reveals, while some related problems are acknowledged and then dismissed, others are ignored altogether. In an episode devoted to pools, the focus is on how pools function as a binding agent for families, are used to advance space exploration, and help the elderly exercise and maintain health. The episode ignores how pools contribute to the water shortages (Gober & Kirkwood, 2010). In an episode about barbecuing, Goldblum explores the mythology of barbecues by bringing up images of the 4th of July and fireworks. He highlights a sense of community around the barbecue and what it does to bring people together; it is a shared experience. What he does not explore are the negative aspects of this type of cooking. For example, many brands of charcoal contain trace metals. Although the emissions of these metals are below government-established thresholds, there are still potential health risks to using these products (Kabir, Kim & Yoon, 2011). There are possible additional environmental and health issues related to the consumption and production of meat. However, these also are ignored in the episode.

In *The World According to Jeff Goldblum*, the negative issues that could be examined in a traditional documentary (or more to the point, a National Geographic-type program) are glossed over or ignored. When problems are addressed, easy solutions to them are offered either through technology or the efforts of hard work. In other words, the problems are framed by a keen sense of optimism and an innocent belief in these conservative and modernist solutions. Or more to the point, Goldblum offers us a perspective in line with the happy, positive view of a "wonderful world." He is not Walt Disney, but he might as well be.

"I Think I'm Done Here"

Tying the history of 20th Century Fox with National Geographic and *The World According to Jeff Goldblum* illustrates the state of The Walt Disney Company and its 21st-century view of media franchising. Disney purchased the iconic film company because of its vast media resources, including the film and television library. The addition of the former company's assets, which included National Geographic, allowed Disney to connect the dots "not merely offering iconic brands across multiple markets, but also formalizing collaborative production across boundaries of the market, production culture, and institutional identity to reproduce culture over time and across media sectors" (Johnson, 2013, p. 233). Yet as Wasko notes, these cultural productions often have a purpose, and she has observed the acquisition of 20th Century Fox and several of the News Corp. assets,

> (R)represents one of the best examples of the synergy that takes place through the cross-ownership of media and entertainment outlets and the recycling of products across these businesses. These moves have provided additional revenue, deepened the demographic appeal of Disney products, and reestablished a positive corporate image.
>
> (2020, p. 262)

Where *The World According to Jeff Goldberg* is concerned, presenting a positive image seems to be the prime motive.

As we have discovered in our analysis, this Disney+ original not only reflects a sense of optimism, but Goldblum delivers this optimism with a sense of discovery, as though he is uncovering the essential truth of the objects and subjects he considers. Considered from the theoretical perspective of cosmopolitanism, the show seems to refigure the practices of banal cosmopolitanism by rendering the banal in cosmopolitan terms. In other words, all the ordinary objects and subjects that Goldblum investigates are revealed to have cultural and social connections that cross cultures, continents, and historical eras. Yet, as we have demonstrated, these investigations are specifically focused on the positive elements and edited to diminish or dismiss any negative aspects. All the while, Goldblum presents his discoveries with the innocent, childlike wonder that Uncle Walt projected in his own anthology shows. In this way, and in contrast to Gina Carano, Goldblum emerged as an employee mindful of and willing to commit to the Disney brand.

As a reward for his efforts, *The World According to Jeff Goldblum* was renewed for a second season and has since been streamed on the Disney+ service. The announcement came only two months after the show debuted. Clearly, Disney liked the show, and although the company has not been very forthcoming with the data it has collected through Disney+ viewership, they saw something they liked. When the renewal was announced on *Deadline*, the president of Content and Marketing for Disney+, Ricky Strauss, had this to say: "Jeff has captured the imagination and curiosity of our audience with his distinct perspective and illuminating adventures. . . We can't wait to see where Jeff and our partners at National Geographic take us in season two" (Hipes, 2020). As we stated earlier, the second season has been uploaded to the service. Its ten episodes run the gamut from dogs and dance to puzzles and monsters. What seems to tie them all together is the connectivity to the Disney brand, and the affable presence of Goldblum does his version of Walt Disney.

We should note that the second season of the show was delayed because like many productions, the pandemic intervened. There have been numerous reports of how scripted productions have established careful protocols and yet still have had to suspend filming because of COVID outbreaks (Fortmueller, 2021). These have occurred in production contexts where cast and crew could be quarantined and isolated on locked down sets and locations. An anthology show like *The World According to Jeff Goldblum* where he travels to various locales and interviews several different people would face additional production challenges.

And that brings us back to the additional challenges that Disney has faced in this pandemic. While Disney confronted some of the same problems regarding film production and exhibition, and other studios like Universal also had to shut down their parks, none of those studios had the same global exposure in the theme park sector. Furthermore, we would maintain that none of those studios has the same brand identity with their parks that Disney has enjoyed. For example, the closure of Disneyland (although other Disney parks may be more popular) had greater significance for the company because it is, in every respect, the original park. It has only been closed twice before, after the assignation of John F. Kennedy and the terrorist attacks on 9/11 (Knowles, 2020). Therefore, the closure also signified an importance not only to Disney but to the US as a whole. In the next chapter, we discuss the ways in which Disney+ served a vital function to connect and engage consumers at a time when those connections and opportunities of engagement were decidedly limited. More specifically, at a time when Disney's parks were closed, Disney+ gave its fans and customers a place to go.

References

Baerg, A. (2015). Exploiting nationalism and banal cosmopolitanism: EA's FIFA World Cup 2010. In Brookey, R., & Oats, T. (Eds.), *Playing to win: sports, video Games, and the culture of play* (pp. 172–190). Bloomington, IN: Indiana University Press.

Beck, U. (2004). Cosmopolitical realism: on the distinction between cosmopolitanism in the philosophy and the social sciences. *Global Networks*, *4*(2), 131–156.

Brookey, R. (2010). *Hollywood gamers: Digital convergence in the film and video game industries*. Bloomington: Indiana University Press.

Brookey, R., & Ecenbarger, C. (2016). Our country, our language, our server: Xenophobic and racist discourse in League of Legends. In Lind, R. (Ed.), *Race and gender in electronic media: Challenges and opportunities* (pp. 179–194). New York: Routledge.

Campbell, G. (2012). *Blood diamonds: Tracing the deadly path of the world's most precious stones*. New York: Basic Books.

Capodagli, B., & Jackson, L. (1999). *The Disney way*. New York: McGraw-Hill.

Chico, D., Aldaya, M., & Garrido, A. (2013). A water footprint assessment of a pair of jeans: the influence of agricultural policies on the sustainability of consumer products. *Journal of Cleaner Production, 57*(15), 238–248.

Claudio, L. (2007). Waste couture: Environment impact of the clothing industry. *Environmental Health Perspectives, 115*(9), A449–A454.

Cotter, B. (1997). *The Wonderful world of Disney television: A complete history*. New York: Hyperion.

Feinberg, D. (2019, November 11). 'The world according to Jeff Goldblum:' TV review. *The Hollywood Reporter*. Retrieved from https://www.hollywoodreporter.com/review/world-jeff-goldblum-review-1253240

Fortmueller, K. (2021). *Hollywood shutdown: Production, distribution, and exhibition in the time of COVID*. Austin, TX: University of Texas Press.

Gober, P., & Kirkwood, C. (2010). Vulnerability assessment of climate-induced water shortage in Phoenix. *PNAS, 107*(50), 21295–21299.

Hanna, J., & Lynch, J. (2019, September 14). An Ohio gamer gets prison time over a 'swatting' call that led to a man's death. *CNN*. Retrieved from https://www.cnn.com/2019/09/14/us/swatting-sentence-casey-viner/index.html

Harvey, C. (2019). What's next for national geographic? a new future for the tv operation after its acquisition by disney. Retrieved from https://www.ft.com/content/bbf5bcce-579e-11e9-8b71-f5b0066105fe

Harvey, D. (1994). Flexible accumulation through urbanization: reflections on 'Post-modernism' in the American city. In Amin, A. (Ed.), *Post-Fordism: A reader* (pp. 361–386). Malden, MA: Wiley.

Hayes, T. (1984, June 20). Rich to sell Fox stakes to Davis. *The New York Times*. Retrieved from https://www.nytimes.com/1984/06/20/business/rich-to-sell-fox-stake-to-davis.html

Hipes, P. (2020, January 17). 'The World According to Jeff Goldblum' renewed for season 2 on Disney+. *Deadline*. Retrieved from https://deadline.com/2020/01/the-world-according-to-jeff-goldblum-renewed-season-2-disney-plus-1202834329/

Iger, B. (2019). *The ride of a lifetime: Lessons learned from 15 years as CEO of the Walt Disney Company*. New York: Random House.

Johnson, D. (2013). *Media franchising: Creative license and the collaboration in the culture industries*. New York: NYU Press.

Jones, C., & Leshkowich, A.M. (2003). The globalization of Asian dress: re-orienting fashion or re-orientalizing Asia? In Niessen, S.A., Leshkowich, A.M., & Jones, C. (Eds.), *Re-Orienting Fashion: The globalization of Asian dress* (pp. 1–48). Providence, RI: Berg Publishers.

Kabir, E., Kim, K., & Yoon, H. (2011). Trace metals contents in barbeque (BBQ) charcoal *Products. Journal of Hazardous Materials, 185*(2, 3), 1418–1424.

Knight, C. (2014). *Power and paradise in Walt Disney's world*. Gainesville: University of Florida Press.

Knowles, H. (2020, March 13). Disneyland closing for third time in history as major theme parks shutter in response to coronavirus. *The Washington Post*. Retrieved from https://www.washingtonpost.com/travel/2020/03/12/disney-is-closing-its-california-theme-parks-coronavirus-precaution/

Kuipers, G., & Kloet, J. (2009). Banal cosmopolitanism and The Lord of the Rings: The limited role of the national differences in global media consumption. *Poetics, 37*(2), 99–118.

Massanari, A. (2017). #Gamergate and The Fappening: How Reddit's algorithm, governance, and culture support toxic technocultures. *New Media and Society, 19*(3), 329–346.

Ogola, J., Mitullah, W., & Omulo, M. (2002). Impact of gold mining on the environment and human health: A case study in the Migori Gold Belt, Kenya. *Environmental Geochemistry and Health, 24*, 141–157.

Rowles, D. (2019, November 12). 'The World According to Jeff Goldblum' is precariously close to too much Jeff Goldblum. *Pajiba*. Retrieved from https://www.pajiba.com/tv_reviews/the-world-according-to-jeff-goldblum-is-precariously-close-to-too-much-jeff-goldblum.php

Said, E. (1978). *Orientalism*. New York: Pantheon.

Saunders, R. (2016). The many facets of Marange's diamonds. In Saunders R., & Nyamunda, T. (Eds.), *Facets of power: Politics, profits and people in the making of Zimbabwe's blood diamonds* (pp. 1–15). Harare: Weaver Press.

Sims, D. (2019, March 21). Hollywood makes way for the Disney-Fox behemoth. *The Atlantic*. Retrieved from https://www.theatlantic.com/entertainment/archive/2019/03/disney-fox-merger-and-future-hollywood/585481/

Solomon, A. (2002). *Twentieth Century-Fox: A corporate and financial history*. Lanham, MD: Scarecrow Press.

Tanigawa, N. (2018, January 16). Proud Boys in Hawai'i. *Hawai'i Public Radio*. Retrieved from https://www.hawaiipublicradio.org/post/proud-boys-hawai-i#stream/0.

The World According to Jeff Goldblum: Season 1. (n.d.) *Rotten Tomatoes*. Retrieved from https://www.rottentomatoes.com/tv/the_world_according_to_jeff_goldblum/s01

Thielman, S. (2015, November 14). How Fox ate National Geographic. *The Guardian*. Retrieved from https://www.theguardian.com/media/2015/nov/14/how-fox-ate-national-geographic

Vary, A. (2020, January 17). Disney drops Fox name, will rebrand as 20th Century Studios Searchlight Pictures. *Variety*. Retrieved from https://variety.com/2020/film/news/disney-dropping-fox-20th-century-studios-1203470349/

Velkey, R. (2016, June 10). Hungarian Roots: William Fox, the man who forgot to sleep and founded 20th Century Fox. *Hungary Today*. Retrieved from https://hungarytoday.hu/hungarian-roots-william-fox-man-forgets-sleep-founds-20th-century-fox-20856/

Wasko, J. (2020). *Understanding Disney* (2nd ed.). Malden, MA: Polity.

Wolff, M. (2010). *The man who owns the news: Inside the secret world of Rupert Murdoch*. New York: Broadway Books.

6 We're Going to Disney+!

This chapter discusses how the feedback and influence between Disney parks and Disney film and TV content has historically been an important part of Disney narratives and branding. We also examine how practices of surveillance deployed in the parks are reintroduced in the Disney+. Finally, the chapter concludes by assessing the place of Disney+ in the broader streaming video market.

After the New York Giants won the 21st Super Bowl in 1987, the teams, their staff, and the news crews covering the game took to the field. Giants quarterback Phil Simms had just been given the Most Valuable Player (MVP) Award, and on-camera, when he was asked what he was going to do next now that he had won the Super Bowl, he replied, "I'm going to go to Disney World!" The video looks spontaneous and unplanned, but it was all part of a carefully constructed ad campaign. According to former Disney CEO, Michael Eisner's memoir, *Work in Progress* (1998), the idea for the campaign came up at a dinner party. In attendance were Eisner, his wife Jane, and George Lucas. Also in attendance were Dick Rutan and Jeana Yeager, a couple who had reportedly been the first to fly non-stop around the globe. Eisner asked these exceptional people who had accomplished this extraordinary feat what they planned to do next. A response came back, "I'm going to Disneyland." Jane turned to her husband and said, "You know, that's a good slogan" (Tan, 2016, para. 8). From that day, an idea to play upon the catchphrase grew. At Super Bowl XXI, it was set up that the player who won the MVP (which ultimately turned out to be Simms), would be converged upon by a camera crew, and out would come those magical words. Since then, every single MVP has said the phrase and has actually gone to either Disneyland or Disney World, except for Super Bowl LV, which was played on February 7, 2021. Although the MVP (Packer's quarterback Aaron Rodgers) recorded the ad, it was reported that the traditional parade featuring the MVP would not be held (Florio, 2021). The pandemic, of course, was the reason for the cancellation.

The success of the campaign is perhaps best illustrated by how it chained out into popular culture. For example, the band Dada released a single in 1992 with the carefully worded title "Dizz Knee Land," in which they

 DOI: 10.4324/9781003364658-6

incorporated the famous saying into a lyric ripe with irony and grunge-era disdain. Five years later, Ellen DeGeneres would mimic the phrase during her television show's famous coming out episode. As Sabrina Mittermeier (2021) has noted, this saying has come to index the significance of the Disney parks to US culture. Indeed, the parks themselves, and Disneyland in particular, have come to index events in our culture, and its closure is a case in point. As we mentioned at the very beginning of this book, the park has only been closed three times in its history; the assassination of JFK, 9/11, and during the COVID-19 pandemic.

The impact of the closure of the Disney parks was more than symbolic to the company, as all of the parks were closed at one time or another during the pandemic. After all, this was a global pandemic. By June 2020, Disney had lost around $6 billion due to the closures (Tate, 2020). These losses are not just due to the lack of ticket, hotel, and food and beverage sales, but also because the parks were an important point of sale for Disney's ancillary products. The closure of the parks also significantly limited that lucrative revenue stream. As we have mentioned before, in addition to the park's closure, cinemas and theaters were also closed, and Disney's cruise ships were docked, so the company lost many opportunities to connect with consumers.

The impact of these closures was also magnified, given the timing of leadership changes at Disney. Unfortunately, about a month before the closures, Iger stepped down as CEO of Disney and had named longtime Disney executive Bob Chapek as the new CEO (Whitten, 2020). Iger cited the acquisition of Fox and the launch of Disney+ as conditions that called for a transition to new leadership. Having been with the company since the mid-90s, Chapek had worked in a variety of capacities for Disney, spanning network television, home entertainment (in the VHS/DVD era), licensing (with a particular focus on integrating Lucasfilm merchandise into the company's roster), and theme parks (Flynn, 2020). Chapek, then, seemed like a logical choice for the post, particularly given the future of the company as imagined by Iger (as discussed in the first chapter). Chapek had experience with the company's parks, which figured prominently in Iger's vision, and he had experience in home video, which would be the market into which Disney+ would be introduced. Despite this experience, he was still an unseasoned CEO when the pandemic hit, and the closure of the parks (and the loss in licensed ancillary sales) significantly eroded the value of his experience. Iger would return to the company in a less prominent role (executive chairman) in April 2020 to shepherd the company through the COVID pandemic and moved his departure date back to the end of 2021 (Goldsmith, 2021).

Fortunately for Chapek and Disney, the Disney+ service would prove valuable for the company during the pandemic. It gave families under lockdown a variety of entertainment options across the company's media brands. It delivered them in a virtual environment in which they could be enjoyed relatively safely. Arguably, the service allowed Disney customers and fans to connect with the company and brand when the opportunities for those connections were few and far between. In fact, on April 20, 2020, Kelly Coffey offered an interesting suggestion on the *Inside the Magic* fan website:

> If you can't go and visit Walt Disney World Resort or Disneyland Resort to see Mickey Mouse or see either Cinderella Castle or Sleeping Beauty Castle in person, we can pop on some Disney+ and stream some shows and films that will make us feel as if we are really there.
>
> (Coffey, 2020, para. 1)

Coffey suggests that Disney+ is a viable substitute for the theme park experience, or to put it another way, the service functions as a virtual theme park, a Disneyland in cyberspace. We agree that even if we could not go to Disneyland or Disney World during the pandemic lockdown, we could all go to Disney+, including Aaron Rodgers.

As objects of academic study go, Disneyland, Disney World, and the other Disney parks have been placed under extensive examination. Some of the most noted studies included Umberto Eco's (1986) assessment of Disneyland as "hyperreal," a space that reproduces places for purposes of consumption. Jean Baudrillard (1994) reaches a similar assessment when he deems Disneyland to be a simulacrum, a constructed space that obfuscates the construction of American experiences. As he observes,

> Disneyland is presented as imaginary in order to make us believe that the rest is real, whereas all of Los Angles and the America that surrounds it are no longer real but belong to the hyperreal order and the order of simulation.
>
> (1994, p. 12)

While this work anchors much of the academic discussion of the Disney parks within cultural studies and critical theory, other disciplines have also engaged the parks. For example, there have been studies of parks from the perspectives of international cultural flow (Van Maanen, 1992; Choi, 2012), organizational culture (Raz, 1999), history (Chytry, 2012; Mittermeier, 2021), consumerism (Dholakia & Schroeder, 2001; Elliott, 2014), architecture (Foglesong, 2001), art history (Knight, 2014), and theater (Allen, 2014). This list goes on, and the body of literature is much too broad to include an exhaustive list. Fortunately, for our purposes, we need only to elaborate a part of that literature, specifically, the concept of remediation.

In their book, *Remediation: Understanding New Media*, Bolter and Grusin (1999) define remediation as the "representation of one medium in another," and they believed remediation was the "defining characteristic of the new digital media" (p. 45). They allow that remediation is not unique to digital media, and they acknowledge Marshall McLuhan's (1964) earlier observations about how the content of a new medium is often an older one. Specifically, McLuhan argued that the content of television drew on film and theater, but the same repurposing of content can be observed in the transition of legacy media companies to digital formats. For example, with the DVD format, major studios found it most profitable to rerelease their back catalogs of film and television shows because the costs of producing that content were often limited to the creation of the digital files (Brookey, 2007). In other words, the DVD drew on content from the old mediums of film and videotape.

Throughout the book, Bolter and Grusin elaborate on the concept of remediation. They do so by identifying various examples of the practice. In a chapter devoted to remediated space, they make a case for both theme parks (Disney parks are singled out) and cyberspace as examples of remediation. Given that the book was published in 1999, they may not have foreseen what would come to pass. After all, DVD was a new consumer technology, and Netflix was a new company based on this technology. While streaming technology was available, the broadband connectivity to make that technology a widely used consumer option was still relatively limited. As we have noted in the preface, however, streaming services would proliferate and serve as their own form of remediation; indeed, Netflix served to remediate the brick-and-mortar video rental store space. We will argue in this chapter that Disney+ is also a remediation of space, but as opposed to the broader offerings of Netflix (and the former video stores), it is more focused on specific brands and the narratives and characters (intellectual property) those brands represent. More to the point, Disney+ is a remediation of the Disney parks.

Our cursory engagement of the literature on the Disney parks is due to the fact that the parks are not our primary object of study. Instead, at the risk of stating the obvious at this point, our object of analysis is the Disney+ service, and we are using the parks as a point of comparison. In this chapter, we will consider how Disney+ functions as a virtual Disney park. We will compare the physical organization of the parks to the interface organization of Disney+, pointing out how narrative spaces are juxtaposed and blended and how the Disney brands are incorporated. We also argue that the Disney+ service replicates the surveillance practices of the parks, thereby rendering those who visit either (or both) as more visible and valuable customers for the company. We then conclude with a summary of the previous chapters and speculate on the media industry's current state (and future) in general.

Disney+, the Virtual Park

The inherent connections between Disneyland and Disney content were clear from the very beginning. After all, the first park was financed by the television deals that Disney struck with ABC, and Disney's earlier televisions show were designed to promote the park and connect it to the studio's content; points we have already established in earlier chapters. In addition, the original Disneyland was built around several themed "lands" that provided structure and organization not only to the theme park experience, but also to the various Disney characters and narratives encountered there. When the park opened in 1955, it was divided into Main Street, Adventureland, Frontierland, Fantasyland, and Tomorrowland. These lands were physical containers that signaled to guests the different themes that also organized the studio's film and television offerings, not unlike how a streaming service uses genres to organize content.

This organizational practice is still present today. "Adventureland," for example, is where guests can go for attractions and stories culled from films as diverse as the Indiana Jones franchise, *Tarzan* (1999), and *Swiss Family Robinson* (1960). Fantasyland has been the home to rides and attractions based on fairy tale characters from Disney films such as *Peter Pan* (1953), *Cinderella* (1950), and *Snow White* (1937). The iconic "It's a Small World" attraction also resides there, a bit ironically, as it frames the intercultural comradery as a fantasy rather than a reality. Mickey's Toontown and Star Wars: Galaxy's Edge are home to, unsurprisingly, attractions based on Disney's library of cartoon characters and all things *Star Wars*.

Disney's theme parks serve a variety of branding and narrative functions as the interconnected, intertextual experiences serve to mediate both stories and consumer experiences. This symbiosis is, of course, the function of Disney+ as well. It is worth noting how the land structure works much like the streaming service's organizational structure. Disney+ uses virtual space to contain and mediate content in ways quite similar to how physical spaces contain and mediate content at Disney theme parks.

The first half-decade or so of Disneyland's existence saw consistent efforts to immerse parkgoers in Disney stories and characters. By 1958, only three years into the park's existence, various attractions invoking Disney television and film properties such as *Davy Crockett* (1955) and *Alice in Wonderland* had been introduced. It is also worth noting that the park featured a Sleeping Beauty attraction two years before the release of Disney's *Sleeping Beauty* (1959) film. This demonstrates that the relationship between Disney's film and television products and its theme parks cuts both ways. The company uses the parks to extend and promote brands, stories, and characters that first enter popular culture through a film or television series. However, there are times where the parks serve as the entry point for a successful Disney franchise, with films or other media content extending the narrative (rather than vice versa). *Sleeping Beauty* is one such early example.

Another example is the *Pirates of the Caribbean* franchise. The Pirates of the Caribbean attraction opened in 1967, not much more than a decade into Disneyland's existence. The attraction was not just a ride or a chance to interact with established Disney characters, or to encounter real versions of fantastic set pieces culled from Disney media properties. Instead, the attraction offered an immersive narrative about pirates plundering the Caribbean Sea. This general story structure formed the basis for the highly successful film series that began in 2003. Of course, the breakout character from the film franchise was Johnny Depp's Captain Jack Sparrow – one of several characters created specifically for the film. The character, though, was added to the theme park attraction in 2006 (Czachor, 2017). In addition, the attraction's Disneyland Shanghai version was revamped in 2016 to reflect the film series (Nolfi, 2016).

Pirates of the Caribbean serves to emphasize a few key points about the role of theme parks in the overall Disney ecosystem. First, it demonstrates that the theme parks are not necessarily just caretakers or promoters of stories or characters from film or television. The Disney theme parks can also originate franchises (and, of course, the accompanying merchandise) with narratives that film or television can extend or expand. Second, there is a narrative and/or branding loop possible in the interplay between Disney theme parks and Disney film and television. The *Pirates of the Caribbean* film series was a spin-off of the ride. But it, in turn, influenced the ride. The process of adaptation, then, reflects on itself, inspiring further adaptations. Finally, *Pirates of the Caribbean* is a reminder that most Disney franchises are about a "long game." The ride was created in 1967, long before a cultural context capable of making a boozy, androgynous, anti-hero pirate a cultural phenomenon. But when that character did become a phenomenon within that cultural context, he was fed back into the Disney theme park experience.

Disney theme parks, then, are not just spaces where Disney characters show up to interact with consumers in a more personal way than is possible on film or television; nor are they just places to buy merchandise. Historically, they can be seen as the immersive, "live" arm for Disney franchises that are otherwise mediated through film and television screens. As we discussed previously, Walt Disney used his television program in the 1950s to keep the public informed about the park's progress, making the show a media space that blended television, film, animation, and theme parks. In 1969, in the lead-up to Disney World's opening, the company released a documentary film about the park's progress (Sampson, 2006), echoing Disneyland's televised opening strategy.

Of course, by the time Disney World opened in 1971, these cross-promotional efforts would continue. Various films about Disney attractions were released and shown at Disney World (a release strategy that evokes a kind of "proto" Disney+ original programming strategy) and then repurposed/released on various television networks. Indeed, there is sustained interplay between Disney theme parks and television throughout the 1970 and 1980s, with all three major networks carrying some kind of Disney content at various times (Disneyland Timeline, n.d.).

Various other events through the 1980s, 1990s, and early 2000s reflect the intertwined nature of the theme parks, various Disney content, and popular culture in general, with noticeable changes along the way because of technological advancements or new Disney partners being brought on board.

As previously noted, Disney theme parks began offering *Star Wars* and Indiana Jones attractions during this era, beginning and then cementing partnerships with Lucasfilm that would culminate in Disney's acquisition of Lucasfilm in 2012. Disney films, both animated and live-action, made their presence felt at Disney theme parks during this period with everything from *Beauty and the Beast* (1991) stage shows to environmental documentaries branded with the *Lion King* franchise, and even a Dick Tracy show. It is perhaps easy to forget the 1990 *Dick Tracy* film (replete with a song about BDSM on its accompanying soundtrack album) fell under the Disney umbrella as their Touchstone Pictures imprint produced it.

It is also worth noting how various attractions have been developed to incorporate the brands and intellectual property that Disney has acquired over the years, and how that intellectual property is related to the content on Disney+. As we noted in the second chapter, Pixar has always had a very close association with Disney. That association can be observed in the park. It's Tough to Be a Bug is a 3D theater attraction drawing characters from *A Bug's Life* (1998), and it has been part of Disney World's Animal Kingdom for 20 years. The Animal Kingdom also houses the Up! A Great Bird Adventure which incorporates characters from the film with a live show featuring performing birds of various kinds. An entire Toy Story Land is housed in Disney World's Hollywood Studio's, and another is housed in Shanghai Disneyland. Ratatouille: The Adventure is housed in Walt Disney Studios Paris, and that park also houses a ride based on the *Finding Nemo* character Crush. Tokyo Disneyland is home to Monsters Inc. Ride and Go Seek and a Buzz Lightyear ride (although that ride also is in Hong Kong Disneyland, Disneyland Paris, Disneyland, and the Magic Kingdom). There are many others we could mention.

As we noted in an earlier chapter, the relationship between Lucasfilm and the Disney parks predates Pixar. The Star Tours attraction opened in Disneyland in 1987 and would later appear at Disney World, Tokyo Disneyland, and Disneyland Paris. The attraction would be refreshed in 2010 as Star Tours: The Adventure Continues. We should also note the presence of Indiana Jones attractions. *Indiana Jones Epic Stunt Spectacular* is a live theater show that opened in 1989. A coaster ride based on the film opened in Paris Disneyland in 1993. Now that Disney owns Lucasfilm, they have opened entire sections of the theme parks devoted to the Star Wars franchise. The Star Wars: Galaxy's Edge are areas that house multiple attractions, and these areas have been opened in Disney World and Disneyland. With these openings, *Star Wars* now demarcates physical space as narrative space, just as the original sections of the original Disneyland.

Marvel, however, has been a bit more challenging where the parks are concerned. Supposedly a preexisting contract with Universal stipulates that Marvel characters cannot appear in any other parks east of the Mississippi. In other words, those characters can appear in Disneyland, but not Disney World (Rasor, 2020). Therefore, Disney is concentrating its efforts to incorporate the Marvel intellectual property elsewhere. Disneyland California Adventure opened an Avengers Campus in 2021, another multi-attraction section of the park similar to the Galaxy's Edge attraction. Additional Avengers Campuses are scheduled for Hong Kong Disneyland and Paris Disneyland. A Marvel-themed hotel also opened at Paris Disneyland, pending progress to contain the pandemic. While none of these attractions will appear at Disney World, it is possible to pick up Marvel merchandise at the Disney Springs area; it is sold at a store discretely named "Super Hero Headquarters."

Finally, there is Fox; although that acquisition has been most recent, and with the shutdown of the parks due to COVID-19, not much progress has been made to incorporate the intellectual property from Fox into the park. Unfortunately for Disney, they face another intellectual property rights challenge from Universal, which has the rights to characters from *The Simpsons* for their own parks (Glenn, 2019). Yet, Disney World has an entire section devoted to Pandora – The World of Avatar. This section of the Animal Kingdom actually predates Disney's ownership of Fox but was undoubtedly part of the discussion when the merger was considered. In other words, with that merger, Disney now had full ownership of the film *Avatar* (2009), and that intellectual property was already incorporated into one of the parks. The film has gone over a decade without a sequel being released – a stunning fact when one considers the commercial success and cultural impact of the film (a sequel was finally released in December 2022). In the absence of a direct sequel, Disney's attraction stood as the direct continuation of the *Avatar,* story and has been essential for extending the film's narrative during that period.

While the parks may have begun to remediate Disney's intellectual property, the practices in the parks have easily accommodated the media brands and properties that the company has acquired over the years. In some cases, Lucasfilm in particular, the parks served as an early entry point for the properties that Disney would acquire. Arguably the parks turned these properties into Disney properties even before they were legally and officially acquired. It is also important to note how these acquisitions have been turned into sections of the parks, providing the same organizational structure of the original "lands" found in the original park. Therefore, the Disney parks have always been organized around narrative spaces, and those spaces have easily transitioned into branded spaces, which brings us back to Disney+.

As we have argued throughout the book, Disney+ blended its various brands into one service but used those brands to organize the service, much in the way narratives and brands have been used to organize the parks. Indeed, the history of the parks and their organization reveal how similar blending has been going on for some time. In addition, the parks created a consumer experience that could be described with qualities often associated with digital media: interactive and immediate. In other words, visitors to the parks could move to and through the spaces at their discretion. Within a matter of minutes, they move from one narrative space to another, much in the manner that people navigate cyberspace. Indeed, the organization of Disney+ also reflects those narrative and branded spaces and replicates the park experience by allowing the same type of interactive and immediate movement. This reflection is not just in the organization of Disney+, but also in the content offered on the service. Therefore, the Disney+ service remediates the park experience, and this may be why Coffey suggested that Disney fans missing the parks can visit the service instead. The connections between the park experience and digital technology, however, do not end here.

The Happiest Surveillance on Earth

Disney recently began articulating its plans to use technology to better foster a union between virtual and physical space – what the company is calling the theme park "metaverse," a term coined by Tilak Mandadi, who serves as Executive Vice President, Digital and Chief Technology Officer for Disney Parks, Experiences and Products (Miller, 2020). In discussing the concept of the metaverse, Mandadi focuses heavily on how customers at theme parks can use their mobile devices to interact with, and engage, the physical environment around them, calling this kind of storytelling "personal" and "social," while casting it as part of an evolution from linear to immersive storytelling. Immersion is, and always has been, a key characteristic of Disney theme parks, with many attractions allowing consumers to interact with characters personally or become parts of narratives themselves. In a pre-digital world, talking to a Disney princess or Mickey Mouse, or helping a rambunctious pirate capture treasure, served as immersion, providing a personal and, as we have noted, interactive experience traditional film and TV could not. The concept of the metaverse, though, suggests the company has something else in mind going forward.

It is also worth noting that the metaverse concept rests on the capacity for Disney to track and record one's movements within the park. This suggests that surveillance and control will continue to be a part of the Disney park experience going forward. Continuing, because both surveillance and control in the parks have been a longstanding Disney strategy. Bryman (2004) outlines how Disney has used various surveillance techniques to keep its employees in line and monitor parkgoers' behavior (and to intervene if necessary). The potential for surveillance and collecting data implicit in contemporary digital technology, then, fits squarely within the

Disney park management strategy – happiness is something that must be carefully controlled and maintained. Therefore, the parks must exercise scrutiny and discipline.

In recent years, Disney has been using "MagicBand" technology. This RFID chip-based wrist band served as a parking ticket, room key, credit card, and general all-around tracking mechanism (Libbey, 2021). For example, when one of us visited Disney World in 2019, he used his "MagicBand" to bypass the check-in desk, access the "Fastpass" lanes, pay for merchandise, and even have the merchandise delivered to his room. We should add that he also had to provide a fingerprint that was matched to the band in order to enter the parks. Of course, such a technology yields access to the kind of financial data implied in any card-based technology, but that financial data now is webbed with the identifying data of a fingerprint. Add to that the ability to constantly track a patron's movement within the park. We see that Disney surveillance practices are deeply layered. In any event, digital technology is just making one of Disney's core impulses easier and more totalizing.

Disney, however, has begun offering alternatives to the MagicBand, including the MagicMobile App, which performs the same functions as a Magic Band, but does it all from a smartphone, generally utilizing technology like Apple Pay (Libbey, 2021). On the Disney World Webpage, customers are also offered a MagicBand+ (following in the branding footsteps of Disney+ perhaps), which in addition to the services offered by MagicBand and Disney MagicMobile, "Unlocks enchanting interactions throughout Walt Disney World." Although the parks already had apps that worked with the Magic Bands, this move to the use of apps and smartphone technology will mainly continue and broaden surveillance and data collection in the parks, and in no way abates privacy concerns. Indeed, the move potentially enables Disney to collect more data about its consumers, as the app on the mobile device will continue to track consumer behaviors outside of the park. The functionality of the MagicMobile App will be contingent on how much access the customer allows, as this was the case with the app tied to the Magic Bands. While guests may decide not to allow the app to access location services on the phone, that most likely will limit the use of the app in practical and perhaps necessary ways. It is common knowledge that the data on our smartphones gets sent out and collected by third parties and used in ways that are not always readily apparent to customers. The MagicMobile app seems likely to function similarly, allowing Disney to collect a great deal of data about its park visitors, including records of their fingerprints.

As we mentioned, the surveillance practices in the parks predate any smartphone technology, and during the early days of Disneyland, Walt Disney even approached the FBI about providing surveillance in the park; they passed on the offer (Mitgang, 1993). The practice of surveillance has also been noted in Disney's employment practices (Giroux & Pollock, 2010).

The use of surveillance by the Disney corporation has been examined in the literature of fields as disparate as law (Richards, 2013) and tourism management (Hollinshead, 1999). Therefore, while surveillance by the Disney corporation is nothing new, the technologies that facilitate and extend the scope of this surveillance are continuing to evolve, and this once again brings us back to Disney+.

Disney+ tracks users like The Magic Bands or MagicMobile. Just as the apps and bands track movement through the parks, Disney+ tracks movement through its service. In both cases, this tracking and the attendant algorithms are designed to collect data in order to tailor a better consumer experience, presumably. The theme parks and Disney+ can strategically navigate a parkgoer or viewer through narratives or toward characters and franchises more effectively. As Jonathan Gray has noted, the data generated in streaming services, however, are often shrouded in secrecy:

> (A)udience data are increasingly proprietary and inaccessible, held by the likes of Netflix, Hulu, Amazon Prime, Facebook, and Google. Occasionally, these corporations may throw scraps of information our way. However, we can neither trust the information nor the reliability of the data dumps. The television audience (and with it all manner of other media audiences) exists behind walls.
>
> (Gray, 2016, p. 79)

While Disney has been very forthcoming with information about subscription numbers, and data that displays the success of *The Mandalorian,* we would aver that these are the very "scraps of information" that Gray references. In other words, Disney does not appear to be more transparent than its streaming rivals, where the granular data it harvests on its users is concerned. We know Disney has a history of exerting a great deal of control over its content and consumers, and it has little compunction about maintaining control through surveillance practices. Disney+ provides another source of data about its customers, produced through the remediation of the park experience in cyberspace. In other words, Coffey's assessment of Disney+ as a virtual substitute for the Disney parks is also valid on a very deep level. We would also suggest, albeit speculatively, that Disney is also closing the loop on that deeper level when they aggregate the data on visitors to the parks with the data it generates on visitors to Disney+. Admittedly this is speculation, but we would argue that it is difficult to imagine Disney passing on the opportunity to enrich their consumer data by forgoing this aggregation; that would be decidedly off-brand.

We began this book by pointing out how the pandemic was one of only three historical events that closed Disneyland. We should note that as of June 30, 2022, the last of the Disney parks to reopen, Shanghai Disneyland, once again welcomed guests. Indeed, these openings reveal that the world has begun to move beyond the pandemic. In 2022 people began returning to theaters, and Disney has two films in the top ten for domestic box office for the year (with *Doctor Strange in the Multiverse of Madness* and *Thor: Love and Thunder*.[1] Summer travel expanded and the theme park business helped Disney post an operating profit for the year (Barnes, 2022). Disney Cruises are up and running, and the company has announced that they will stop testing fully vaccinated passengers (Thomaselli, 2022). Although they were significantly impacted by the pandemic, it appears Disney has survived and arguably, thrived. That survival can be attributed, in no small part, to the Disney+ service. When housebound families scrambled for entertainment options; Disney+ was there, even when all of its other entertainment offerings were shut down. Indeed, now that the effects of the pandemic seem to have subsided, Disney+ seems to be competing with Netflix while other streaming services seem to still be struggling (Barnes, 2022).

Is Disney the Disruptor?

We did not anticipate the pandemic when we began the research for this book. Instead, we were interested in how Disney was going to deploy its various brands for the Disney+ service. With the introduction of the service, Disney had to be strategic about the content, which informed our decision to analyze the original content that appeared at the launch of Disney+. Again, this content was not created in response to the pandemic, as it was all produced before the pandemic. Instead, it was created to draw upon intellectual property that could be re-purposed for new media distribution systems (Bettig, 1996). What we have discovered in our research is that Disney+ successfully navigated the pandemic and the emergence of the streaming market by remaining fully Disney; both in terms of the content itself, and the production of that content.

In fact, our first chapter revealed how the business practices that Iger imagined would refigure and prepare Disney for the transition to streaming were not only already in place, but they could also be traced back through the company's history beginning with Walt Disney. Historically, Disney has been a company that has cultivated a variety of content, explored new technologies, and globalized the company brand through a variety of entertainment offerings and products. Therefore, Disney+ is one of the latest manifestations of these practices. In terms of the content itself we found the Disney+ original content reflecting the Classic Disney style, story, characters, themes, and values (Wasko, 2001). In other words, Disney launched Disney+ with content that was decidedly Disney's. In addition, our analyses went deeper, connecting this original content to important contexts and histories related to Disney and their brands.

For example, Pixar was always closely associated with the Disney Company, and that association was primarily due to John Lasseter's presence at both companies. However, in 2017, he had to take a "leave of absence" from the company due to charges of sexual misconduct and creating a "culture where women and people of color do not have an equal voice" (Barnes, 2017, para. 9). While his departure solved the problem in the short term, Disney still had to repair the brand. Enter Purl, a female ball of pink yarn who overcomes toxic masculinity at a company called B.R.O Capital. While some praised the short film for its feminist take on the workplace culture, we discovered how the film was very problematic with how it portrayed an easy solution to a complex problem. In this regard, *Purl* was a Classic Disney film; yet given the specific details of Lasseter's behavior at Pixar, the short suggests that the social circumstances in which B.R.O. Capital's culture is refigured are similar to those in which Lasseter was at his most predatory. As we point out, *Purl* does a better job of protecting the Disney and Pixar brands than truly addressing toxic masculinity in the workplace. *Purl* signals that Pixar (and by association Disney) understands the problem women encounter in a work environment and understand the importance of a supportive place for diversity in the workplace. Unfortunately, as a "feminist allegory," *Purl* provides few valuable clues to how an accepting and supportive workplace can be achieved.

Young people have always been at the core of The Walt Disney Company. *Marvel's Hero Project* production as a Disney+ original was designed to connect with that core. Our analysis relates *Marvel's Hero Project* to *The Mickey Mouse Club*, as both shows were intent on showcasing exceptional young people and offering them as representatives of the media brands. We identified various similarities between *The Mickey Mouse Club* (focusing on the episodes of the original series that were placed on the service for the launch) and *Marvel's Hero Project*. For example, both shows required the embodiment of the brands; the Mouseketeers wore the iconic mouse ears, and the Marvel kids were rewarded (and encouraged to don) the Marvel superhero jacket. Just as The *Mickey Mouse Club* would reward inductees with a box of branded products, so too does *Marvel's Hero Project* award its members a Marvel branded box.

Yet, the most notable similarity is the way the later program reproduces the economies of the former. Both programs draw on the actual identities of these young people as it reconstitutes them as brand ambassadors, and in doing so, Disney and Marvel establish a level of ownership over those identities as intellectual property. It also obtained that intellectual property by offering minimal compensation. As we note, *The Mickey Mouse Club* derived great value from the Mouseketeers by paying the talented members of this club union scale wages. *Marvel's Hero Project* recreates its subjects as comic book characters, using the show to illustrate how each young person is a "hero" in their own right. Yet, Marvel (and Disney) retains intellectual property rights for this content. The end credits for *Marvel's Hero Project* states that "all characters featured in this issue and the distinctive names and likenesses thereof, and all related indicia are trademarks of Marvel

Characters Inc." This means that the "hero" is now licensed intellectual property of Marvel and, therefore, Disney.

The Mandalorian could be called the first Disney+ megahit. At its heart, the series appeals to a fan base specialized in *Star Wars* culture. We noted in our analysis the various ways the show provides fan service. Yet, we contextualize our analysis of the historical relationship between Lucasfilm and Disney. While some of that relationship was stylistic (*Star Wars Holiday Special* is a case in point), it would eventually become a business relationship. Lucasfilm intellectual property began appearing as attractions in the Disney parks. In addition, we addressed the fan revolt against *Star Wars* creator George Lucas as another important context through which to critique *The Mandalorian*. As we noted, this chapter departed a bit from our standard practices, as our analysis also extended to the paratextual series *Disney Gallery: The Mandalorian*. By analyzing both series, we discovered how the practices of fan service were purposeful and how true Star Wars fans were incorporated into the production of the series. We also discovered another purpose regarding Lucas and his legacy, as those involved in making *The Mandalorian* pay allegiance to Lucas while also asserting their own agency in the continuation of the Star Wars saga. More to the point, the series illustrates that the Star Wars universe is now in the hands of people who are themselves fans, who respect Lucas and his contributions but are willing to move the franchise forward with their own stories. As for *The Mandalorian* itself, the Disney+ original plays into the Disney brand with a redemption narrative that suggests there is always hope. Through selfless actions, like those of Din Djarin, we can all persevere.

We would never have chosen Jeff Goldblum to serve as a new surrogate for Walt Disney, but no one asked us. Disney and National Geographic chose differently when it came to producing original programming for the Disney+ service. *The World According to Jeff Goldblum*, we argued, is a contemporary manifestation of the anthology program that brought Walt Disney into viewers' homes in the 1950s and 1960s (Capodagli & Jackson, 1999). We note that the term "world" is used a lot in different manifestations of these Disney anthology shows, reflecting the broad scope for the series. Hence, it made sense that after the purchase of 21st Century Fox and the National Geographic brand by Disney, that later brand would serve to introduce a new anthology show on the Disney+ service. Thus, *The World According to Jeff Goldblum* was born.

As we noted, the show's premise is Mr. Goldblum exploring the everyday world of topics such as sneakers, ice cream, and coffee, by tracing their origins and their broader cultural implications. Our analysis revealed that while a thorny issue may be thrown in during the program, these problems are quickly dispatched. Indeed, problematic elements associated with these objects appear in Goldblum's worldview briefly, if they appear at all (the economic and social impact of jewels and precious metals are overlooked, for example). In the conclusion of each episode, Jeff Goldblum discovers an essential truth about the object in question, always ending on an optimistic note. Although Goldblum offers us a view of the world, it is through a decidedly Disney lens. Drawing on theories of banal cosmopolitanism, our analysis demonstrated how Goldblum's investigations, while tracing these ordinary objects through history and across continents, render simplistically optimistic conclusions. Jeff Goldblum as the host of his program, is certainly not Walt Disney, but his anthology show is decidedly a Disney product.

Finally, in this chapter, we discussed how the Disney+ service provides remediation of the Disney theme park experience. The service is the cyberspace manifestation of the variety of narrative and branded spaces experienced and explored in the parks. The service provides the cyberspace equivalent of the surveillance practices of the park, rendering Disney fans as data points to reconstitute them as better (more compliant) Disney customers. Therefore, the Disney+ service became a destination point that replaced and reproduced the parks during the pandemic in transparent and clandestine ways. Moving forward, however, it is clear that Disney+ will strategically serve as a surrogate for the parks. During his presentation to the latest D23 Expo in Anaheim, Chapek had this to say:

> Disney+ will not just be a movie service platform . . . it's going to become an experiential lifestyle platform. A platform for the whole company to embody both the physical things that you might be able to experience in a theme park, but also the digital experiences that you can get through media.
>
> (Patten, 2022, para. 3)

We began this project with questions about Disney and its various brands, and we illustrated in our analyses how the original content analyzed successfully integrated these brands. We cannot attribute that success of the service to the specific programming we analyzed, though arguably, *The Mandalorian* proved a significant draw. However, our analyses reveal the overarching strategy that may have contributed to the success of Disney+. The service successfully deployed the various brands because the shows related to those brands were, in the final analysis, Disney products. Indeed, the Disney+ service has most likely attracted and retained subscribers because it offered up precisely the type of content people associate with Disney.

In other words, Disney entered the streaming market, and has succeeded thus far by remaining Disney. Given all the rhetoric about the streaming wars, and the disruption of a media market by streaming services, the story of Disney+ is quite different. Disney, as both a company and a brand, has remained relatively undisrupted. In fact, it could be argued that Disney has proven to be the disruptor. Although the lead that Disney took over Netflix was a relatively slim one million subscriber margin, the impact on Netflix has been much more significant. Netflix has financed its original content production by taking on an extraordinary level of debt, while never turning a profit. When the service was still growing its subscriber base and besting the competition in total subscribers, investors seemed unbothered by this debt load. Now that Netflix is actually shedding subscribers, and no longer dominating the market in total subscribers, Wall Street has started to think differently. In 2022 Netflix lost 60% of its market value, as investors began to question the company's practices and its ability to face increased competition (Klebnikov, 2022). As was reported by Josef Adalian (2022) in *Vulture*: "'The world changed because of what happened with Netflix,' one industry wag says. Absent a road map for profitability, 'you can't just spend $20 billion on content anymore.'" In other words, moving forward, streaming services are now going to be held to the traditional standards imposed on the stock value of companies, those involving profitability.

Although the Disney+ service may not yet be profitable itself, Disney as a company is performing quite well given that all of its points of vulnerability during the pandemic (parks, cruises, theatrical releases) have now become points of sale. In other words, Disney's business practices of diversification, practices that we traced in the first chapter, are driving Disney's bottom line, and allowing them to best the competition, specifically Netflix. Again, Disney is succeeding in the streaming era because of practices that have always been in place. Disney is winning by being Disney.

Yet, Disney's disruption may be broader in that its presence may be reconstituting the streaming service market into something that looks very familiar. Netflix made a market space for itself through disruption. It disrupted the video rental film market by eliminating late fees and providing high-profile and high quality direct-to-streaming films (Scorsese's *The Irishman*, 2019, is a case in point). It had also disrupted television by eliminating ads and releasing the full seasons of series at once. These disruptive practices, however, have themselves been recently disrupted. Netflix announced last year that it will begin releasing some series episodes on a weekly basis and announced this year that they are partnering with Microsoft to offer advertisements. The direct-to-streaming film releases that were necessitated by the pandemic, are now giving way to a reemergence of the theatrical release. Furthermore, these more traditional practices for both television and film releases, and the incorporation of advertising, are emerging across many of the streaming services including Disney+.

Therefore, the streaming era moving forward is starting to look like the old broadcast media environment, with a handful of companies releasing content on a weekly basis, often supported by advertising revenue. We should note that these practices were already in place on the Hulu service, a service for which Disney was an early partner. Others have made similar observations about the future of the streaming market. In an article in *The Washington Post*, TV writer and producer Tim Doyle observed,

> The streaming services are moving more toward becoming more similar to broadcast networks and cable networks that existed before. . . They've suddenly come up with this great idea that if you put in advertising, you can make money selling the ads! So they're just kind of retreating back to the things that are familiar.
>
> (Andrews, 2022, para. 8)[2]

Therefore, the legacy of Disney+ and its entry into the streaming market may be to lead the competition back to the business practices that were in place in the early years of television, a period in which Disney had already established an important presence.

As we tentatively emerge from the pandemic, and as normal media consumption practices return, we are still faced with an uncertain future in the streaming market. Undoubtedly streaming will survive and flourish as a mode of home video delivery; no one is uncertain about that. However, how many of these services will survive, though in what form is unknown, and reorganization and new alliances are still being formed: Paramount+ is teaming with Walmart+; Warner Bros. Discovery is merging HBO Max with Discovery+, etc.

We feel that we can say with some certainty that Disney+ will have a future, because as a company it has not lost sight of its past. On the contrary, we believe the service is successful because it reasserted the Disney brand in this new market, producing original content that reflects the Disney Style, and maintaining practices that have always served the company for several decades. While we are uncertain if Disney will continue to prove to be a disruptor of the streaming service market, we are certain they have emerged as an important force in this market, and have done so by remaining Disney, undisrupted.

Notes

1 Again, box office data was retrieved from Boxofficemojo.com.

2 We should note that Doyle isolates an important difference that remains in the streaming era, and that is in regard to talent compensation, particularly for writers. Streaming series often have small episode orders, meaning that writers are continually looking for their next job, rather than enjoying the security of a full season network order. In addition, the streaming era has significantly eroded the revenue generated by syndication, and this revenue stream was important to talent compensation.

References

Adalian, J. (2022, August 10). The HBO Max rumor mill was wrong – but there's still pain to come. *Vulture*. Retrieved from https://www.vulture.com/2022/08/the-hbo-max-rumors-were-wrong-but-theres-still-pain-ahead.html

Allen, D. (2014). Disneyland: Another kind of reality. *European Journal of American Culture*, *33*(1), 33–47.

Andrews, T. (2022, September 7). Streaming TV is having an existential crisis, and viewers can tell. *The Washington Post*. Retrieved from https://www.washingtonpost.com/arts-entertainment/2022/09/07/streaming-tv-changes-crisis/

Barnes, B. (2017, November 21). John Lasseter, a Pixar founder, Takes Leave After 'Missteps.' *The New York Times*. Retrieved from https://www.nytimes.com/2017/11/21/business/media/john-lasseter-pixar-disney-leave.html?_r=0

Barnes, B. (2022, August 10). Disney profit jumps 50%, and streaming subscriptions surpass Netflix. *The New York Times*. Retrieved from https://www.nytimes.com/2022/08/10/business/disney-earnings-profit.html

Baudrillard, J. (1994). *Simulacra and simulation*. Ann Arbor, MI: University of Michigan Press.

Bettig, R. (1996). *Copyrighting culture: The political economy of intellectual property*. Boulder, CO: Westview Press.

Bolter, J., & Grusin, R. (1999). *Remediation: Understanding new media*. Cambridge, MA: MIT Press.

Brookey, R. (2007). The format wars: Drawing the battle lines for the next DVD. *Convergence, 13*(2), 199–211.

Bryman, A. (2004). *The Disneyization of Society*. Thousand Oaks, CA: Sage Publishers.

Capodagli, B., & Jackson, L. (1999). *The Disney way*. New York: McGraw-Hill.

Choi, K. (2012). Disneyfication and localization: The cultural globalization process of Hong Kong Disneyland. *Urban Studies, 49*(2), 383–397.

Chytry, J. (2012). Walt Disney and the creation of emotional environments: interpreting Walt Disney's oeuvre from the Disney studios to Disneyland, CalArts, and the Experimental Prototype Community of Tomorrow. *Rethinking History, 16*(2), 259–278.

Coffey, K. (2020, April 20). Missing the Disney parks? Watch these Disney+ shows and Films. *Inside the Magic*. Retrieved from https://insidethemagic.net/2020/04/disney-plus-missing-disney-parks-kc1/

Czachor, Emily Mae. (2017, July 7). Disneyland's Pirates of the Caribbean: 50 years of change. *The Los Angeles Times*. Retrieved from https://www.latimes.com/entertainment/la-ca-mn-disneyland-pirates-timeline-20170707-htmlstory.html

Dholakia, N., & Schroeder, J. (2001). Disney: Delights and Doubts. *Journal of Research for Consumers*, 2. Retrieved from http://jrconsumers.com/Academic_Articles/issue_2/DholakiaSchroeder.pdf

Disneyland Timeline. (n.d.). *California State University, Sacramento*. Retrieved from https://www.csus.edu/indiv/s/shawg/articles/facilities/disneyland_timeline.html

Eco, U. (1986). *Faith in fakes: Travels in hyperreality*. New York: Harcourt Brace Jovanovich.

Eisner, M. (1998). *Work in progress*. New York: Random House.

Elliott, K. (2014). Tie-intertextuality, or intertextuality as incorporation in the tie-in merchandise to Disney's Alice in Wonderland. *Adaptation*, 7(2), 191–211.

Florio, M. (2021, February, 5). This year's Super Bowl MVP won't be going to Disney World. *NBC Sports*. Retrieved from https://profootballtalk.nbcsports.com/2021/02/05/this-years-super-bowl-mvp-wont-be-going-to-disney-world/

Flynn, K. (2020, February 25). Who is Bob Chapek, Disney's new CEO. *CNN*. Retrieved from https://www.cnn.com/2020/02/25/media/bob-chapek-bio-disney/index.html

Foglesong, R. (2001). *Married to the mouse: Walt Disney World and Orlando*. New Haven, CT: Yale University Press.

Giroux, H., & Pollack, G. (2010). *The Mouse that roared*. Lanham, MD: Rowman & Littlefield.

Glenn, B. (2019, March 25). Let's talk about the Simpsons rights at Universal parks. *Inside Universal*. Retrieved from https://www.insideuniversal.net/2019/03/lets-talk-about-the-simpsons-rights-at-universal-parks/

Goldsmith, J. (2021, March 9). Bob Iger bids Disney shareholders farewell at his last annual meeting. *Deadline*. Retrieved from https://deadline.com/2021/03/disney-bob-iger-annual-shareholders-meeting-1234710204/

Gray, J. (2016). Reviving audience studies. *Critical Studies in Media Communication, 34*(1), 79–83.

Hollinshead, K. (1999). Surveillance of the worlds of tourism: Foucault and the eye-of-power. *Tourism Management, 20*(1), 7–23.

Klebnikov, S. (August 22, 2022). Netflix is not the worst performing stock in the S&P 500 as shares plunge over 60% in 2022. *Forbes*. Retrieved from https://www.forbes.com/sites/sergeiklebnikov/2022/08/22/netflix-is-now-the-worst-performing-stock-in-sp-500-as-shares-plunges-over-60-in-2022/?sh=4023f3da7ac7

Knight, C. (2014). *Power and paradise in Walt Disney's world*. Gainesville, FL: University of Florida Press.

Libbey, D. (2021, March 30). Walt Disney World just took a major step toward ending Magic Bands. *CinemaBlend*. Retrieved from https://www.cinemablend.com/news/2565095/walt-disney-world-just-took-a-major-step-toward-ending-magicbands

McLuhan, M. (1964). *Understanding media: The extensions of man*. New York: McGraw-Hill.

Miller, K. (2020, November 16). Disney's Tilak Mandadi: Using technology to transform storytelling in the Disney metaverse. *The Global Association for the Attractions Industry*. Retrieved from https://www.iaapa.org/news/funworld/disneys-tilak-mandadi-using-technology-transform-storytelling-disney-metaverse

Mitgang, H. (1993, May 6). Disney link to Hoover and FBI is disclosed. *The New York Times*. Retrieved from https://www.nytimes.com/1993/05/06/movies/disney-link-to-the-fbi-and-hoover-is-disclosed.html

Mittermeier, S. (2021). *A Cultural History of the Disneyland Theme Parks*. Bristol, UK: Intellect.

Nolfi, J. (2016, May 11). Shanghai Disneyland: Pirates of the Caribbean Battle for the Sunken Treasure POV video. *Entertainment Weekly*. Retrieved from https://ew.com/article/2016/05/11/shanghai-disneyland-pirates-caribbean-ride-video/

Patten, D. (2022, September 10). Bob Chapek details Disney's next bi move, the 100th anniversary, ESPN & Hulu's futures, & bringing "Everything Together." *Deadline*. Retrieved from https://deadline.com/2022/09/disney-bob-chapek-interview-100th-anniversary-plans-espn-hulu-1235114628/

Rasor, D. (2020, April 17). Why Disney World will never get its own Avengers Campus. *All Ears*. Retrieved from https://allears.net/2020/04/17/why-walt-disney-world-wont-be-getting-its-own-avengers-campus/

Raz, A. (1999). The hybridization of organizational culture in Tokyo Disneyland. *Culture and Organization, 5*(2), 235–264.

Richards, N. (2013). The dangers of surveillance. *The Harvard Law Review, 126*(7), 1934–1965.

Sampson, W. (2006, October 25). Walt Disney World's first press event. *Mouse Planet*. Retrieved from https://www.mouseplanet.com/8165/Walt_Disney_Worlds_First_Press_Event_1969

Tan, A. (2016, February 3). How 'I'm going to Disney world!' began as post-super bowl slogan. *ABC News*. Retrieved from https://abcnews.go.com/Business/im-disney-world-began-post-super-bowl-slogan/story?id=36605612

Tate, C. (2020, August 6). Disney lost nearly $5 billion while the theme parks were closed due to coronavirus. *USA Today*. Retrieved from https://www.usatoday.com/story/travel/2020/08/04/disneys-theme-park-coronavirus-closures-result-hit-3-5-billion/3292766001/

Thomaselli, R. (2022, August 31). Disney Cruise line eases COVI9–19 testing requirements. *Travel Pulse*. Retrieved from https://www.travelpulse.com/news/cruise/disney-cruise-line-eases-covid-19-testing-requirements.html

Van Maanen, J. (1992). Displacing Disney: Some notes on the flow of culture. *Qualitative Sociology, 15*(1), 5–35.

Wasko, J. (2001). *Understanding Disney* (1st ed.). Malden, MA: Polity.

Whitten, S. (2020, February 25). A look at Bob Iger's legacy as he steps down as CEO. *CNBC*. Retrieved from https://www.cnbc.com/2020/02/25/disney-ceo-bob-iger-steps-down-a-look-at-his-legacy.html

Index

For Product Safety Concerns and Information please contact our EU
representative GPSR@taylorandfrancis.com
Taylor & Francis Verlag GmbH, Kaufingerstraße 24, 80331 München, Germany

www.ingramcontent.com/pod-product-compliance
Lightning Source LLC
LaVergne TN
LVHW021131300926
849160LV00010B/960
* 9 7 8 1 0 3 2 4 2 8 6 7 3 *